# *Strategies for Sustainability*

## *Africa*

MW
SL
MWEAR

9700177020

## IUCN: The World Conservation Union

Founded in 1948, The World Conservation Union brings together states, government agencies and a diverse range of non-governmental organizations in a unique world partnership. IUCN has over 895 members in all, spread across some 137 countries.

As a Union, IUCN seeks to influence, encourage and assist societies throughout the world to conserve the integrity and diversity of nature and ensure that any use of natural resources is equitable and ecologically sustainable. A central Secretariat coordinates the IUCN programme and serves the Union membership, representing their views on the world stage and providing them with the strategies, services, scientific knowledge and technical support they need to achieve their goals. Through its six commissions, IUCN draws together over 6000 expert volunteers in project teams and action groups, focusing in particular on species and biodiversity conservation and management of habitats and natural resources. The Union has helped many countries prepare National Conservation Strategies and demonstrates the application of its knowledge through the field projects it supervises. Operations are increasingly decentralized and are carried forward by an expanding network of regional and country offices, located principally in developing countries.

IUCN builds on the strength of its members, networks and partners to enhance their capacity and support global alliances to safeguard natural resources at local, regional and international levels.

## The Strategies for Sustainability Programme of IUCN

Based on the principles of the World Conservation Strategy and *Caring for the Earth*[1], IUCN supports the preparation and implementation of strategies for sustainability in response to requests from governments, communities and NGOs. The Strategies for Sustainability Programme of the IUCN Secretariat and the Working Group on Strategies of the IUCN Commission on Environmental Strategy and Planning (CESP) assist those involved in strategies through a programme aimed at:

- undertaking conceptual development and exchange and analysis of experience concerning strategies throughout the world;
- carrying out demonstration and testing of key elements, tools and methodologies in strategies;
- building regional networks of strategy practitioners; and
- strengthening local capacity by engaging the networks in conceptual development, exchange and analysis of experience, and demonstration activities.

The programme draws on experience with all types of strategies regardless of their sources of support. Working group members include practitioners in national conservation strategies, national environmental action plans, other national strategies, international strategies, and a wide range of provincial (state) and local strategies.

1. IUCN, UNEP and WWF (1991). *Caring for the Earth: A Strategy for Sustainable Living.* Earthscan Publications, London.

5043008

# Strategies for Sustainability

## Africa

*Adrian Wood, Editor*

*Strategies for Sustainability Programme*

SHORT LOAN

UNIVERSITY OF GREENWICH LIBRARY

333.
7150
96
STR

IUCN

The World Conservation Union

Earthscan Publications Ltd., London

*Strategies for Sustainability: Africa* was made possible by the generous support of the Swedish International Development Authority, the International Development Resource Centre (IDRC) and the Swiss Agency for Development Cooperation (SDC).

First published in the UK in 1997 by:
Earthscan Publications Limited, in association with IUCN

Copyright © International Union for Conservation of Nature and Natural Resources, 1997

Reproduction of this publication for educational or other non-commercial purposes is authorized without prior permission from the copyright holder. Reproduction for sale or other commercial purposes is prohibited without the prior written permission of the copyright holder.

A catalogue record for this book is available from the British Library

ISBN: 1 85383 270 7

Design: Patricia Halladay

Earthscan Publications, 120 Pentonville Road, London N1 9JN, UK
Tel: 0171 2780433   Fax 0171 2781142
Email: earthinfo@earthscan.co.uk
Web site: http://www.earthscan.co.uk

IUCN Publications Services Unit, 219c Huntingdon Road, Cambridge CB3 0DL, UK
IUCN Communications Division, Rue Mauverney 28, CH-1196 Gland, Switzerland

The views of the authors expressed in this book, and the presentation of the material, do not imply the expression of any opinion whatsoever on the part of IUCN concerning the legal status of any country, territory, or area, or concerning the delimitation of its frontiers or boundaries.

Printed and bound in the UK by Biddles Ltd., Guildford and King's Lynn

Printed on acid- and elemental chlorine-free paper, sourced from sustainably managed forests and processed according to an environmentally responsible manufacturing system.

UNIVERSITY OF GREENWICH
17 MAR 1998
LIBRARY

# Contents

## Malawi

## Nigeria

## Serengeti

## Tanzania

## Preface

This publication is part of an IUCN series of Regional Reviews of Strategies for Sustainability covering Asia, Africa and Latin America. The series is devoted to an analysis of lessons learned in multi-sectoral strategies at national, provincial and local levels. It aims to assemble and analyze experience in the development and implementation of strategies so that strategy practitioners and agencies may improve future strategies.

The series of regional reviews is a joint undertaking by the Strategies for Sustainability Programme of The World Conservation Union (IUCN) and its Commission on Environmental Strategies and Planning (CESP). It was carried out in cooperation with other organizations, such as the International Institute for Environment and Development (IIED), the World Bank, the United Nations Development Programme (UNDP), the World Resources Institute (WRI) and, in the case of this Africa review, the Network for Environment and Sustainable Development in Africa (NESDA).

The regional reviews cover only a sample of case studies in each region, recognizing that all the experience that a region has to offer can never be captured in a single volume. The case studies were compiled between 1993 and 1995, depending on the availability of strategy teams and information. Most case studies cover the period up to late 1995, although a few end a little earlier.

The case studies are not intended to be evaluations. They are analytical histories of strategies, providing a summary of basic information and lessons learned by the teams who have developed the various strategies. The case studies presented in this volume were prepared by the members of the strategy teams across Africa with the assistance of an IUCN resource team. The authors met together first in 1992 at a workshop at Lake Baringo in Kenya; many of them met again in September 1995 to revise and update the case studies at the Africa Regional Strategies Workshop in Ethiopia.

It is important to emphasize that much of the work undertaken in these cases represents pioneering efforts in strategic planning and implementation. The learning value of the workshops was greatly increased by the participants' willingness to discuss their experiences frankly and openly. They focused on problems they encountered, on lessons they had learned, and considered their failures as opportunities to learn.

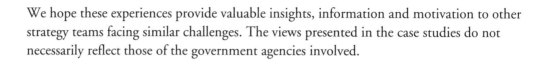

We hope these experiences provide valuable insights, information and motivation to other strategy teams facing similar challenges. The views presented in the case studies do not necessarily reflect those of the government agencies involved.

## *Acknowledgements*

IUCN wishes to thank the authors of the case studies and workshop participants for giving so freely of their time and experience in order to share with others the lessons they have learned through perseverance and trial and error. They were supported in their work by an IUCN Resource Team for both the Baringo and Ethiopia workshops. The Lake Baringo Workshop Resource Team included Jeremy Carew-Reid, Nancy MacPherson, Robert Prescott-Allen and Adrian Wood for IUCN, and Steven Bass and Barry Dalal-Clayton of IIED. The Ethiopia Workshop Resource Team included Julius Chileshe, Alejandro Imbach, Nancy MacPherson and Adrian Wood for IUCN and Mangetane Khalikane of NESDA.

We are particularly grateful to Dr. Adrian Wood for his work coordinating the information for these case studies and for editing this volume.

We are also grateful for the financial support from the Swedish Development Authority (SIDA) and the United States Agency for International Development (USAID), which supported us in organizing and hosting the workshops where these case studies were discussed and analyzed, and to the Swiss Agency for Development Cooperation (SDC) for the funds to publish and distribute this volume.

Local arrangements for the Baringo and Ethiopia workshops were made by the IUCN Office for Eastern Africa (EARO) in Nairobi, Kenya. The Ethiopia NCS Secretariat in Addis Ababa provided assistance with local arrangements for the Ethiopia workshop. To the staff of these offices we extend our thanks for their able assistance.


Nancy MacPherson
Coordinator
Strategies for Sustainability Programme
IUCN HQ
Gland, Switzerland

# Synthesis and Analysis

## 1 Overview

This volume reviews more than a decade of experience with strategies for sustainability in 12 African countries (see Table 1). These countries provide examples of very different approaches to strategy development and implementation. Many (Guinea-Conakry, Kenya, Lesotho, Malawi, Nigeria, Uganda, Zambia) have been involved in the development of National Environmental Action Plans (NEAPs) at the request of the World Bank. Other countries have developed their strategies independently (Eritrea, Nigeria and Zimbabwe), or have prepared National Conservation Strategies (NCSs) with support from IUCN (Botswana, Ethiopia, Tanzania, and Zambia).

Until recently the majority of strategy experience in Africa has been at the national level. But with the growing recognition that local-level strategies provide a means of connecting national policy frameworks with action on the ground, many countries in Africa are embarking on local-level strategies. This volume reviews 15 national strategies and three local strategies, the local initiatives being a nationally developed strategy for environment and development in a specific ecological zone in Kenya's arid and semi-arid lands; a protected area based sub-regional strategy in the Serengeti (Tanzania and Kenya) and the District Environmental Action Planning Process in Zimbabwe.

## Table 1. African Strategies Reviewed in this Volume

| Country/area | Date | Type of strategy |
|---|---|---|
| Botswana | 1984 | National Conservation Strategy (NCS) |
| Eritrea | 1994 | Environmental Management Plan (EMP) |
| Ethiopia | 1989 | National Conservation Strategy (NCS) |
| Guinea-Conakry | 1989 | National Environmental Action Plan (NEAP) |
| Kenya | 1990 | Environmental Action Plan for Arid and Semi-Arid Lands (EAP-ASAL) |
|  | 1993 | National Environmental Action Plan (NEAP) |
| Lesotho | 1988 | National Environmental Action Plan (NEAP) |
| Malawi | 1992 | National Environmental Action Plan (NEAP) |
| Nigeria | 1983 | National Conservation Strategy (NCS) |
|  | 1991 | Environmental Management Plan (EMP) |
| Serengeti | 1989 | Serengeti Regional Conservation Strategy (SRCS) |
| Tanzania | 1989 | National Conservation Strategy for Sustainable Development (NCSSD) |
|  | 1993 | National Environmental Action Plan (NEAP), |
| Uganda | 1991 | National Environmental Action Plan (NEAP) |
| Zambia | 1984 | National Conservation Strategy (NCS) |
|  | 1993 | National Environmental Action Plan (NEAP) |
| Zimbabwe | 1983 | National Conservation Strategy (NCS) |
|  | 1994 | Zimbabwe District Environmental Action Planning Process (DEAP) |

## 2 Strengths and Weaknesses

Analysis from the case studies in this volume — and the discussions at the 1992 Lake Baringo workshop and the 1995 Ethiopia workshop where the case study material was presented — provides a preliminary framework of strengths and weaknesses in current strategy practice. These are summarized in the following section. The strengths and weaknesses raise a number of issues which are discussed in Section 3; Section 4 provides some guidance towards best practice.

Participants of the Lake Baringo and Ethiopia workshops, in presenting the experience of their countries in developing and implementing strategies, were encouraged to be as introspective and analytical as possible in order to maximize learning from their experience. They were assisted by a technical resource team from IUCN. The team provided a case study format which set out a framework designed to highlight the lessons learned and minimize unnecessary details.

At the 1995 Ethiopia workshop, the IUCN Resource Team noticed a marked increase in the capacity of teams to highlight lessons learned, compared with the first meeting of strategy teams at Lake Baringo in 1992. This can be attributed to a number of factors:

- many strategy teams now have up to a decade of experience upon which to reflect (for example, Zambia, Botswana, Zimbabwe);
- many strategies have moved from the development phase into implementation, with the common pitfalls and flaws in strategy processes becoming more evident as time passes; and
- there is less inter-institutional tension and more ability and willingness to reflect on the strategies in general, rather than on NCSs or NEAPs in particular.

The following charts set out the range of strengths and weaknesses identified by participants. These topics are not in order of importance, but appear in the order raised in the discussion.

*Development and Implementation Phases*

**Conceptual/Contextual**

*Key pitfalls/weaknesses*

- lack of clear vision of sustainable development
- limited awareness of sustainable development issues among civil society
- not using previous strategy initiatives as the contextual starting point
- failure to invest in training and capacity-building from the start
- implemented under political/social instability
- frequent political changes during implementation

*Strengths*

- strong support at political level
- awareness created about sustainable development and environmental issues as a result of the initiative
- high level of government and political commitment

## Process

*Key pitfalls/weaknesses*

- too much focus on document production; lack of practical action and field demonstration from the start
- the rush to produce a document compromises the development of widespread involvement of stakeholders
- excessive use of external consultants weakens local capacity development
- failure to take a strategic view and identify key priority issues
- poor/limited information flow during preparation
- lack of demonstration and action simultaneous with the development phase
- lack of management capacity in the development and implementation phase
- limited participation from the outset and lack of capacity to sustain participation throughout the process
- lack of emphasis on communication capacity, in particular communication for behaviour change
- poor or inadequate feedback to the public, probably due to lack of communication and information systems
- long lag between strategy preparation, government approval and implementation leads to loss of momentum and staff
- only one official language used in the final document even where several written languages were accessible to local communities

*Strengths*

- enabled government agencies and other stakeholders to participate in international events and workshops
- private sector participation in process and activities established new relationships and links
- initiated dialogue between stakeholders about sustainable development
- encouraged participants, including government, to focus on priority issues
- phasing implementation activities leads to a gradual build-up of skills

## Institutional

### *Key pitfalls/weaknesses*

- lack of integration in key economic and development planning policies, programmes and processes
- inadequate institutional framework for preparation of the strategy
- limited cross-sectoral coordination and sharing of resources
- fragmentation of responsibilities for the preparation of the strategy
- weak or nonexistent district-level involvement
- institutional and legal aspects handled too late in the process
- conflict resolution mechanisms not in place
- frequent changes in the institutional framework

### *Strengths*

- strengthened local capacity for strategy development
- created new national environmental institutions and legislative and policy frameworks
- facilitated institutional capacity-building
- enabled the government to coordinate donor activities and support
- integration with the national planning and development institutional process
- many agencies and institutions have to collaborate for implementation

**Analytical Content**

*Key pitfalls/weaknesses*

- inadequate economic analysis; natural resource accounting weak or nonexistent in most NCSs and NEAPs

- inadequate social analysis

- lack of cross-sectoral focus

- too comprehensive; too much analysis and data; lost track of the main issue

- lack of strategic focus in analysis

- absence of needs assessment for implementation leads to stalling of the process

- failure to consider current programme investments

- failure to formulate strategies at a realistic level for local capacities and resources, thus creating unrealistic expectations

- limited use of past experience of and/or failure to use indigenous knowledge for baseline information

*Strengths*

- several strategies acted as a catalyst for rigorous and innovative economic and social analysis

- generated valuable information and baseline data

## Funding

### *Key pitfalls/weaknesses*

- inadequate/erratic funding of phases produces a stop/start impact, resulting in a loss of momentum and skills
- donor-driven in many cases
- lack of donor coordination
- project funding approach to the ESP leads to a fragmentation and failure to keep the strategic focus, thus the process disintegrates into fragmented projects
- inadequate government commitment to the implementation of strategies leaves donors reluctant to fund the whole initiative

### *Strengths*

- integrated approach to donor support can provide an umbrella initiative for environmental programming
- the process can assist governments to mobilize financial and technical support resources internally and externally

## Monitoring and Evaluation (M&E)

### *Key pitfalls/weaknesses*

- most strategies have inadequate monitoring and assessment mechanisms, either internal or external

### *Strengths*

- in rare cases M&E is a priority and provides a process to ground the strategy

## 3 Current Issues

Detailed analysis of the experience in developing and implementing strategies in Africa raises a number of questions and issues for current practice in strategies.

### Pre-conditions

*What are the minimum requirements which must be met in a country before a strategy is undertaken?*

Case studies indicate that pre-conditions for the successful development and implementation of a strategy include political support, at least some environmental awareness among civil society and government, a core of skilled and committed people, a clear concept or vision of sustainable development and relatively peaceful conditions under which to take action.

#### Assessment of Preconditions

Governments and sponsoring agencies need to assess whether the preconditions for success have been fulfilled before commencing a strategy process. Where these are not met, either a strategy should not be attempted, or consideration should be given to a preliminary stage to help fulfil the preconditions. In Guinea-Conakry, where the strategy process began without these preconditions, major difficulties were experienced in the development phase.

#### Political Support

Strong political support is needed to ensure access to the information, resources and means to implement strategy actions. This is especially important where there is a lack of cooperation between government departments. Political intervention may be required to ensure that inter-departmental rivalries are put to one side and that government departments cooperate in the strategy process. Developing a consensus on the vision for the strategy and the necessary path of action is especially important in strategy processes, which tend to be particularly cross-sectoral and inter-ministerial in nature. Political support must also ensure that there is effective participation from all sectors and from civil society. The Zimbabwe NCS and the Kenyan Environmental Action Plan for Arid and Semi-Arid Lands both suffered from a lack of political approval and support, which hampered implementation.

#### Awareness

Support for a strategy is facilitated by a level of awareness about environmental problems and their solutions. This awareness may come about as a result of severe environmental problems, as has been the case with soil erosion in Kenya and Ethiopia; or because of severe economic conditions which force a country to make greater use of its natural resources, as in Zambia; or by concerted efforts in environmental education. The experience of a military struggle may also help introduce new leaders to environmental issues, as was the case in Zimbabwe, Uganda, Ethiopia and Eritrea.

*Timing*

The timing of an environmental strategy process can be critical. Developing a strategy when other issues dominate the political agenda can create difficulties in gaining the support and resources necessary for action. This was the case with the Zimbabwe and Zambia strategies in the late 1980s, when post-war reconstruction and economic adjustment, respectively, held the governments' attention. On the other hand, the UNCED Earth Summit at Rio provided a focal point for environmental concerns among national governments, donors and international organizations and acted as a catalyst for many environmental initiatives.

It can be counter-productive to force strategy processes on countries that are not ready to act. Considerable resources and human efforts were wasted in the start-up of the NEAP in Guinea-Conakry because the timing was premature for a full-blown strategy process. In contrast, in Ethiopia the strategy process specifically fought against pressures to produce a national strategy quickly and instead built a national framework for action slowly and steadily.

*Core Groups and Vision*

An environmental core group composed of representatives with relevant technical and political skills from government, NGOs and business can assist in providing both an 'engine' and a vision for the process. Core group members can carry out a number of functions, such as lobbying for a strategy process, making links with key community, NGO and technical groups, and undertaking strategy formulation and implementation. The group can also ensure that the strategy's momentum is maintained during periods of limited political support or change in governments.

Using task forces in strategy processes in Africa is an adaptation of the core group concept that was first developed in Nepal. In Zambia and Zimbabwe such groups have helped ensure that strategies developed in the 1980s have not been forgotten, and that they made progress in the 1990s when political and economic conditions became more favourable. In Eritrea a task force of government staff, who were given responsibility for the formulation of the Environmental Management Plan, developed a vision for the strategy process and helped to drive it forward.

## Institutional Arrangements

*Which institution(s) should initiate the strategy? Where should it be located and what powers, linkages and responsibilities should it have?*

### Strategy Location

Strategies should be located at a sufficiently high level within government to ensure that environmental issues are considered in all aspects of national development. This may require location in, or close to, the Office of the President or Prime Minister, or within the institution responsible for development planning. Such an arrangement, which has been sought by some NEAP and NCS processes, has been successful in providing access to power, thereby leading to faster political approval and more effective implementation.

### Sectoral Location Problems

Experience shows that, where strategies are initiated within a single sectoral agency, such as a Ministry of Environment or a research body, they are often marginalized and fail to gain the support of other key ministries. This may stem from the position of environmental ministries in the political hierarchy, and their limited external linkages and powers. In this situation, an environmental strategy tends to be treated as another line ministry or sectoral initiative, rather than as a broad multi-sector support initiative.

### Cross-Sectoral Linkages

The strategy secretariat must establish strong institutional linkages not only with development planning and other line ministries, but also with the private sector and communities. Such links are often constrained by the lack of awareness of the connection between environment and development factors. This seems to have been the case in several of the countries studied, especially Zambia, Zimbabwe and Tanzania, where there has been little involvement by the planning and development agencies and private organizations in strategy formulation.

### Coordination Capacity

The strategy secretariat should have powers of coordination across sectors as well as the ability to work at the sub-national level. Without such a mandate the secretariat will be seriously hampered. While there are many cases where strategies lack coordination powers (e.g., the NCSs in Tanzania, Zambia and Zimbabwe), there are also some encouraging examples. One is in Ethiopia where the NCS has coordination powers both through the Office of the Prime Minister, where policy issues are considered, and through the Ministry of Economic Development and Cooperation, where the day-to-day coordination of the different ministries is undertaken.

Another way to provide coordination is by establishing environment liaison officers or environmental units in line ministries (as is the case in Botswana, Eritrea and Lesotho). In Botswana, a specific coordinating role is assigned to the strategy secretariat. However, there are few examples of institutionalized links outside government. Among these case studies, Lesotho provides the only example of formal coordination of the strategy with NGOs.

## Scope, Type of Strategy and Harmonization

*What should be the scope of the strategy? What type of strategy is sought? How can the various demands of different environmental strategies be met and integrated?*

### Proliferation of Strategies

There are increasing demands on countries to prepare and implement strategies of various types. These demands will increase with the new National Action Programmes against Desertification (NAPs) and Biodiversity Action Plans introduced by the Desertification and Biodiversity conventions. It is worthwhile for countries to take a long-term view when setting up a strategy process so that it can address the requirements for a number of strategies without having to duplicate processes and drain scarce human resources. The scope of the

strategy should be wide enough to provide a basis for future requirements such as biodiversity action plans, Agenda 21 plans and NAPs. There is some evidence of developments in this direction in Tanzania and in Lesotho, where Agenda 21 requirements have been incorporated into their existing initiatives.

### Focus on Sustainable Development

Breadth and flexibility in a strategy process can be achieved if a sustainable development (SD) approach is taken. Whatever the specific focus of the strategy may be, it should take as its starting point the country's SD goals, recognizing that it is not possible to have healthy ecosystems without healthy people — at least not in the long term. Using an SD focus as an umbrella or framework for the strategy allows for the further development of specific requirements to meet the needs of conventions (Biodiversity, Montreal Protocol, CITES) and international agreements such as Agenda 21 without duplicating the baseline work.

### Avoiding Replication and Parallel Processes

In order to avoid wasting time and effort, countries should rationalize and consolidate their involvement in strategy processes. This requires them to be assertive with agencies who pressure them to start parallel or similar strategy processes. The principle of building on previous initiatives should be the basic premise for countries and agencies interested in additional strategies. An example is Ethiopia, which successfully convinced the World Bank to accept its National Conservation Strategy as an NEAP equivalent. The Ethiopia NCS also acts as an umbrella strategy for the Forestry Action Plan, the Strategy to Combat Desertification and Agenda 21.

It is equally important to build on sector master plans, e.g. in forestry, water and energy. NEAPs and NCSs should be seen as frameworks which can incorporate these plans or strategies and provide them with crucial inter-sectoral linkages. In this way value can be added to the plans that sectors themselves produce. There is evidence of this in a number of countries, especially in Kenya, where sectoral strategies have contributed to both the NEAP and the EAP for Arid and Semi-Arid Lands.

### Harmonization of Strategies

In several countries there have been problems of duplication, with different national-level environmental strategies, such as NEAPs and NCSs, competing for resources. Tanzania, Zambia and Nigeria have had varying experiences with attempts to integrate and harmonize these different national strategy processes, although institutional rivalry has been common in all cases. Harmonization can, in fact, be a disincentive for countries in

that taking on new strategy processes often provides new and often needed human and financial resources. This factor must be recognized by agencies who encourage governments to take on a variety of strategy processes.

## Sustaining and Internalizing the Strategy Process

### How can the process be sustained and internalized?

#### Local Control and Ownership

Many strategy processes are one-off events and are never internalized within governments, NGOs or communities. For strategies to be sustained they must have widespread support among civil society, NGOs and government at different levels in the country. This will only be achieved if strategies empower people and meet the needs and priorities articulated by the population.

The strategy's initiation and support is crucial. Experience in Africa shows that, in many cases, strategies have been imposed upon countries with very limited local control over the resulting process and products. This is particularly true of NEAPs. The situation has been challenged by some countries, however, and there is now an increased recognition of the need for local control. Examples of strong local involvement include Kenya's EAP for the

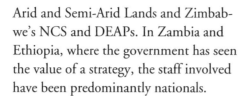

Arid and Semi-Arid Lands and Zimbab-we's NCS and DEAPs. In Zambia and Ethiopia, where the government has seen the value of a strategy, the staff involved have been predominantly nationals.

### Awareness

In general the cases studied have not involved activities such as sensitization, awareness and capacity-building from the outset, but have focused on data collection and document production. An investment by the strategy process in fostering and enhancing public awareness of environment and development factors and linkages can help to ensure a greater degree of local ownership over the process.

Strategy processes that offer tools and guidance to help agencies and people achieve their goals will be more easily internalized. However, as the Zambian NCS shows, care must be taken not to present a distorted picture of the costs or benefits of strategies.

### Integration

The overall economic conditions in a country can affect the integration of strategies into the development planning process. Integration may be especially difficult where economic problems are severe and macro-economic considerations predominate in development planning. This has been the case in a number of countries, most notably Zambia, where the implementation of macro-economic

policies and structural adjustment are proving especially difficult.

## Process and Participants

*What process should be followed and who should be involved?*

### Conceptual Framework for the Strategy Process

A clear understanding of the purpose and objectives of the strategy process should precede the commencement of strategy activities. A lack of such understanding has often led strategy teams and participants to focus on the production of the strategy document rather than on the capacity-building processes required to carry out the actions.

### Balancing Activities

In a strategy process it is important to maintain a balance between data collection/analysis and process/capacity-building. A document or investment programme should not drive the process at the expense of the development of skills necessary to carry out the strategy and establish an ongoing process.

Some NEAP processes have experienced difficulty in this regard because the production of the NEAP document has been a requirement for IDA loan replenishment. Document production has tended to dominate the process at the expense of capacity-building and skills development. On the other hand, strategies which have not concentrated on a rigorous, documented analysis end up with an inadequate data base upon which to make decisions. Time and resources must be committed to all phases: documentation, building a process and constituency, and capacity-building.

*Strategies as a Cyclical Process*

Previous planning experience has often led to a conception of a strategy as linear, with a clear separation of the development phase and implementation phase. The practice of strategies following separate, discrete phases is widespread in Africa. Strategies should instead be thought of as cyclical processes, with an iterative cycle of assessment, analysis, policy formulation, implementation, reflection and monitoring and assessment, leading to readjustment of actions.

Notable exceptions to the linear model are the Serengeti Regional Strategy and the Zimbabwe DEAP process, where a cycle of assessment and action is encouraged in the preparation of the strategy action plans or documents.

*Momentum*

Many strategies have seen lengthy delays between the development and implemen–tation phases (linear model) or in the approval stage of the strategy document. This has led to a loss of momentum and loss of staff from the Secretariat and a general decline in the profile and effectiveness of the strategy process. This is seen in most of the case studies in this volume, although it is especially clear in the Lesotho, Zimbabwe and Kenya (EAP-ASAL) cases.

To maintain momentum and support, it is often helpful if strategies initiate imple-mentation or demonstration activities which offer benefits to the community and build up momentum and support. This can be achieved more easily if strategies do not rely entirely on new funds and activities, but instead focus some of their efforts on existing investments and activities.

*Mechanisms for Integration*

Strategy processes can use a range of options to achieve their aim of integrating environmental considerations into the development process. In some cases, such as the Tanzanian NCSSD, there is a tendency to focus on planning mecha-nisms. Policy formulation, demonstration activities, technical and financial mecha-nisms, legal measures, communications and education are other ways to move the strategy along.

*Strategic Approach*

A strategy cannot address all issues at once; it must be strategic in terms of scale and priority. Early in the process it is useful to determine what the key issues will be for resource users and managers.

Because the perception of key issues will vary among the users and managers, national strategies will need to be seen as frameworks which are further articulated at a regional or local level by communities and administrators.

## Participation in Strategy Processes

### The Need for Participation

In most of the case studies, the strategy processes include some form of consultation but have very limited ongoing participation. In the case of the Nigerian NCS, the Serengeti Regional Strategy and the Kenyan EAP for ASAL the strategies were drafted almost entirely by government technical experts, with little ongoing involvement of local officials, NGOs or communities. In most cases there has been some form of nominal consultation, with the draft strategy discussed with selected representatives of local government and communities. A more inclusive process is needed which provides an opportunity for input from communities at a early stage before the basic framework of the strategy becomes fixed.

In Uganda and in Botswana, in contrast, there was much more active participation and widespread discussion of what was needed in the strategy before drafting took place. This involved discussions at the village level with community groups who presented ideas before the framework was set.

### Stakeholder Analysis

While experts may think they know who should be involved in strategies, it is often useful to carry out a stakeholder analysis of the region, province or country in which the strategy is being prepared to determine who are the users and the managers, who controls economic power and decision-making, land tenure and so on. The results of a stakeholder analysis will give a profile of the groups that need to be represented in a strategy process.

### Problem-solving Through Participation

Participation by the public can help identify solutions to problems identified in the strategy by drawing upon local knowledge. Similarly, the involvement of professional organizations, the private/business sector and NGOs, each with their own perspectives, may help identify solutions. It is recommended that participation include those who do not agree with the strategy goals as well as those who do. This allows the strategy to anticipate the major obstacles to successful implementation, engage fully in conflict resolution at an early stage, and overcome major obstacles which can stop it from moving forward at a later stage.

### Barriers to Participation

Participation can be constrained by a number of factors. Inter-departmental politics and rivalry can create institutional barriers. Fears over personal security and the absence of open democratic processes may discourage people from cooperating, and may prevent a creative approach to developing options for sustainable development. External pressures from donors or international agencies — who may push for 'products', such as investment programmes, before the strategy process has had the time to develop — will also militate against participation.

Real participation (beyond consultation) is costly and time consuming. If participation is to be successful the institution initiating the strategy must have the mandate, time and resources to sustain it.

### Reality of Participation

Involving everyone in a strategy formulation process is an overwhelming and impossible task. Thinking in terms of optimal levels of participation, recognizing that the optimal will vary from case to case, may help to find an appropriate level of participation. Participation needs to target groups and to apply methods suited to local conditions. Equity issues should also be considered so that particular groups are not disenfranchised.

## Scale and Level of Operation

### Local-level Strategies

Over the past decade most strategies in Africa have been initiated at the national level. Recently, however, there has been a shift towards local-level strategies that link with national frameworks. Ethiopia, with

conservation strategies for each of its regions, and Zimbabwe, with its District Environmental Action Plans (DEAPs), are examples of attempts to establish local-level strategic initiatives to 'ground' national strategies. Local action plans can also provide demonstrations of action and behaviour change, and can build up momentum among resource users. In Lesotho, Uganda, Nigeria and Tanzania the need for local articulation of strategies has been recognized. Further developments towards sub-national strategies can be expected in other parts of Africa as governments move towards a more decentralized form of managing resources.

### Regional and River Basin Linkages

The case studies from Lesotho, Botswana, Zimbabwe and Eritrea refer to the need to link national strategies with international initiatives, including regional, coastal, catchment and basin strategies. Initiatives involving the Zambezi Basin and Red Sea are cited as regional examples, while recent efforts to address desertification in the Save Catchment area in Zimbabwe is an example at the sub-national level.

## Skills and Capacity

### Skills Assessment

Experience shows that insufficient attention has been given at the start of strategy processes to assessing a country's skills and capacities. Ignoring the need for local capacity-building often leads to too much reliance on consultants and external agencies. This may lead to 'over-building' of strategy processes based on unrealistic views about the capacity of local institutions. This will make strategy processes dependent on external assistance and not locally sustainable.

### Capacity Development

Building skills should be a major focus of strategy development and implementation. The pace of the strategy process should allow for any necessary skill development in order to enhance capacity for the implementation phase. The Zambian and Ethiopian cases report considerable capacity-building in the strategy process, and little use of external consultants. This helped ensure that the Zambian strategy kept going through the difficult times in the late 1980s, and allowed the Ethiopian strategy to survive the change of government in 1991. In contrast, in Guinea-Conakry – and to a lesser degree in Botswana and Lesotho – shortages of skills had been particularly restricting for strategy work.

## Outputs

### Types of Outputs

The intended output of the strategy needs to be carefully considered at the outset. It may include a strategy document, legislation, policies, an investment programme, institutions, demonstration activities, skill

development and capacity-building. All of these are legitimate 'products'. Different constituents will want different products. Politicians and decision-makers will look for legislative and policy changes; community participants will want to see concrete action on the ground and training. It is important to have a forum in which to determine the balance between different outputs.

### The Nature of Outputs

In order to facilitate approval and implementation, attention should be given to the nature of the outputs. These need to be of immediate use and must be easily understood by those who will approve them and use them. The strategy document, for instance, must be suitable for consideration by the politicians who will approve it. In Zambia the strategy document was concise and focused on the key issues. This helped to get it onto the Cabinet's agenda. Any legislation developed should address priority needs in the country and try to ensure that benefits are produced for as wide a section of the community as possible.

Many strategies neglect awareness-raising and focus primarily upon the technical, legislative and institutional aspects. A strategy process may need to begin with communication and educational activities that will raise awareness or with field activities which address immediate and clearly visible problems. This was the case in Ethiopia, where advice on land-use planning was an initial point of contact which led to the country's National Conservation Strategy. Similarly in Kenya, Uganda and Tanzania, projects related to the management of game parks, wetlands and protected forests were the initial activities which raised awareness of the value of strategies.

## Mechanisms for Implementation

The steps to full implementation may include:

- official approval of the strategy as the country's agenda for environmental programming;
- key legislation and policy changes involving the full range of stakeholders;
- institutional arrangements and mandate for a coordinating body such as planning commissions; and
- clarification of the roles of all relevant ministries and NGOs in implementation.

### Action Plans

Action plans have now become recognized as essential for facilitating implementation. Many of the early strategies (for instance, the NCSs in Zambia and Zimbabwe) suffered from a lack of specific action plans. This resulted in slower implementation of the strategy recommendations, which were sound but often vague.

### Driving Force

Strategies need an 'engine' to drive the process: an organization, institution or NGO with vision and energy. Consideration should be given early in the process to whether the strategy secretariat will remain in place to assist in implementation and undertake monitoring and evaluation. Disbanding the secretariat means losing the corporate memory of the process, and if there is no other 'engine' to drive the implementation forward the process could stop. This has been a problem at times in Lesotho and in Kenya with the EAP-ASAL when the merger of government ministries took place.

### Opportunistic and Strategic Implementation

In the implementation phase it is important to find a balance between being opportunistic (in order to get activities underway), and being strategic (which may mean spending more time in developing those activities which are central to the strategy). Donor influence may lead to an over-emphasis on bankable projects, rather than a focus on a broader programme/process/and capacity-development approach. This can lead to major gaps, which can cause the strategy to collapse. This type of problem appears to be developing with the Environmental Support Programme (ESP) phase of NEAPs, where there is selective funding of the projects by donors.

## *Monitoring and Evaluation (M&E)*

To date, most of the strategy processes reviewed have little emphasis on monitoring and evaluation, also known as assessment. A notable exception is the Zimbabwe DEAP, which has an internal M&E methodology at the heart of its strategy and action planning. The Botswana NCS and the Lesotho NEAP report plan to develop environmental management systems and state-of-the-environment reports, which will provide data on the impact of strategy initiatives.

Two different levels of M&E need to be considered in strategy processes: monitoring and assessing the condition of the environmental system and the people within it; and M&E of the strategy itself. System assessment is concerned with the state of ecosystems and human development, and self- and project assessments are concerned about the way in which projects and institutions are taking action to respond to the state of ecosystems and people. These must be clearly differentiated and understood. External assessments required by donors usually relate to the delivery of project outputs and do not focus on system assessment.

It should be stressed that monitoring and assessment is a key element of the continuous strategy cycle, where reformulation of the strategy occurs in the light of reflection on the strategic action undertaken. M&E provides the methods and tools to determine key sustainability needs and issues, set priorities, and develop baseline indicators for measuring progress.

## *Funding*

### *The Need for Domestic Funding and Self-Reliance*

Strategies are often perceived by governments and stakeholders exclusively as a source of new funds, with no emphasis on what people can do for themselves, or what adjustments need to be made to existing activities. This is often the case with NEAPS, where a loan portfolio is a major focus of the strategy, but other strategies are just as vulnerable. If this happens then strategies can end up as wish lists of projects which can never be locally sustainable and which rely on large infusions of external funds.

There must be a clear financial commitment from the government. This is important for two reasons. First, the strategy process might not be sustainable if it is funded at a high level by external donors who may suddenly cut their support. Second, it is important that the process is understood and supported domestically. This is more likely if the government is making a financial commitment.

The experience of Eritrea provides a good example of government commitment. The Environmental Management Plan was produced almost entirely from domestic resources in response to a domestic initiative. The experience with unpredictable donors, particularly in the Serengeti strategy, suggests that reliance upon donors should be minimized as much as possible.

*Investment Analysis*

It is important for participants to realize that the strategy process is not solely about projects and obtaining new funds. Rather, the process should be first and foremost about behavioural change. It should help people to determine what they can do for themselves first, without any funds, and then how to make better use of existing resources (human and financial) through investment analysis of ongoing activities. Only after this analysis should consideration be given to which additional resources are required to take further action.

*Coordination of Funding*

Coordination of donor funding is also necessary to ensure that competitive activities are not initiated. In Ethiopia the government has ensured that donors accept the coordinating role of the National Conservation Strategy (NCS). As a result there is a growing level of collaboration among the government and donor-supported environmental activities under a clear framework provided by the NCS.

## 4 Towards Good Practice in Strategies

Analysis of the experience of the various African strategies has contributed to the development of general recommendations concerning the development and implementation of strategies. These can be found in detail in the *Handbook on the Development and Implementation of National Strategies for Sustainable Development* (IUCN, IIED 1995). A number of key lessons can be highlighted.

### Conceptual Framework for the Strategy

Key stakeholders must have a clear understanding of sustainable development goals and of the problems of unsustainable use of resources. If they don't, it is worth investing in an awareness-raising programme prior to strategy start-up. It may also be necessary to undertake research to better understand the motivation behind unsustainable resource use practices.

### The Strategy Process

A clear understanding must be developed about the cyclical nature of the strategy process and its different aspects:

- assessment of needs;
- analysis of information and data;
- priority setting and action planning;
- awareness raising;

- document production;
- investment activity identification; and
- capacity development, etc.

The range of outputs and their relevance to different stakeholders must be recognized. The strategy process should be 'country-driven' and owned, with a minimal presence of outside agendas. It should strive to sustain the participation of key players, not just carry out one-off consultations.

### Institutional Arrangements

Strategy effectiveness is influenced by the level of political and institutional commitment from key institutions. From an early stage a strategy 'engine' should be developed that is linked to (or has influence over) the development planning system. This should ensure cross-sectoral linkages between key environmental sectors, such as parks, marine, fisheries, and other levels of society and government education, media, health, extension services and economic development.

### Technical Components

The strategy process should include assessment of both ecosystem and human well-being. This will require an assessment process that deals equally with biodiversity and state-of-the-environment information as well as human development information. Gaps in the data should be filled through participatory assessments with stakeholders, but should not involve data-heavy research.

Key linkages between people and ecosystems must be analyzed and understood in order to properly address cause-and-effect relationships and understand resource use and dependence. Analysis of the economic and social linkages with environment should be undertaken to help understand the effects of macro-economic policies, like structural adjustment, public sector reform policies and cultural views. This should include the use of indigenous knowledge systems.

### Monitoring and Evaluation

A self-monitoring and evaluation methodology should be developed as part of the strategy process. It should be used to ensure that needs are properly assessed in the first place, and to make sure that strategy actions are on-track and readjusted according to reassessments as the strategy evolves. Are the needs assessed accurately in the first place? Are the actions of the strategy addressing these needs? If not, what adjustments are needed? Are there improvements in ecosystem and human well-being? If not, why not?

### Funding

The strategy process must be funded and staffed at a sustainable level over the long term, and must avoid high levels of inputs (financial and professional) that cannot be maintained. Financial arrangements should include reliance upon domestic government resources as well as external donors. A mechanism for coordinating and educating donors will be needed. Sustainable financing mechanisms, such as trusts and National Environment Funds, should be developed. Rather than always looking for new funding, strategy teams should refocus existing resources, or, if those resources aren't working, cancel them. Use should be made of the pyramid-of-action approach, where the emphasis is on what people can do for themselves.

### Demonstration Activities

Strategies should emphasise demonstration activities to facilitate understanding and awareness, and to help build support and capacity. There should be action-oriented demonstration activities on the ground early in the strategy process.

*Information for the chapter title pages was taken from the following publications:*

a) Human Development Report 1995, United Nations Development Programme, Oxford University Press, New York.

b) The Cambridge Encyclopaedia, David Crystal, Ed., Cambridge University Press, 1990.

Information on Eritrea was taken from the National Environmental Management Plan for Eritrea, Government of Eritrea, January 1995.

In some instances, additional information was also taken from The New Encyclopaedia Brittanica: Micropaedia, 1992.

# *Botswana*

*National Conservation Strategy*

STEVIE C MONNA, NATIONAL
CONSERVATION STRATEGY
(COORDINATING) AGENCY

**Estimated population 1992:** 1.4 million;
**Land area:** 567,000 km²; **Ecological
zones:** land-locked, undulating sand-filled
plateau, dry scrubland and savannah, and
Kalahari Desert; **Climate:** largely
subtropical, increasingly arid in south and
west; **Annual rainfall:** 200–450 mm;
**Forest and woodland area:** 108,900 km²;
**GNP per capita:** US$2,450; **Main
industries:** subsistence farming, minerals,
mining, livestock products and tourism;
**ODA received per capita:** US$79.9;
**Population growth rate (1992–2000):** 3
per cent; **Life expectancy at birth:** 64.9
years; **Adult literacy rate:** 67.2 per cent;
**Access to safe water:** 89 per cent; **Access
to health services:** 89 per cent; **Access to
sanitation:** 55 per cent

## 1 Introduction

The Government of Botswana recognized the need for the preparation of a National Conservation Strategy (NCS) in 1983. The NCS emerged from a report known as the 'Clearing House Mission' which was produced through close cooperation between the government and the United Nations Environment Programme (UNEP), and which identified the need for policies and other measures ensuring, wherever and whenever possible, the sustainability of all future development.

The issues of environment and development which led to the formulation of the NCS related to land degradation, rangeland degradation, wildlife depletion and management, and the depletion of wood resources and veld products as well as water resources. The underlying concerns were that the quality of these resources were in danger of being reduced and that, consequently, they would not be adequate to support economic development in the future.

Against the above background, the Government of Botswana requested technical assistance from IUCN for the preparation of the NCS with financial assistance mainly from the Norwegian Agency for Development Cooperation (NORAD), the Swedish International Development Authority (SIDA), the EEC and the Government of the Netherlands.

The NCS was adopted by Parliament in December 1990 as Government Paper No 2: 'National Policy on Natural Resources Conservation and Development'.

## 2 Scope and Objectives

The strategy is national in scope and primarily aims at pursuing policies and measures focused on the following areas:

- increasing the effectiveness with which natural resources are used and managed, so that the beneficial interactions are optimized and harmful environmental side-effects are minimized;
- integrating the work of the many sectoral ministries and interest groups throughout Botswana, thereby improving the development of natural resources through conservation, and vice versa;
- the development of new sustainable uses of natural resources and optimization of existing uses of natural resources;
- the development of multiple, rather than single-purpose uses of natural resources and the diversification of the rural economy;
- the increased education and participation of all members of society in improving the environment;
- the establishment of a balance between population growth and the supply of natural resources;

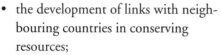

- the development of links with neighbouring countries in conserving resources;
- the conservation of all main ecosystems, wildlife and cultural resources;
- the protection of endangered species;
- the maintenance of stocks of renewable resources (eg veld products), while increasing their sustainable yields; and
- the control of the depletion of exhaustible resources (eg minerals) at optimal rates.

## 3 Preparation of the NCS

The preparation of the NCS for Botswana has been carried out in two phases. The first phase was concerned with the development of the policy framework which articulated the overall strategic goals as well as the framework and measures which should enable key environmental issues to be addressed effectively. It also aimed at identifying the institutional and legislative measures that are required for the successful implementation of the NCS.

The government and IUCN have worked jointly on the NCS since 1984. The preparation of the NCS involved a broad consultation process which was undertaken at all levels of society in Botswana, including central government and parastatal officials, local government officials, members of the non-governmental organization (NGO) community, private sector companies, district councillors, members of acadaemia, traditional leaders and communities.

While a number of recommendations from the first phase have been implemented, the strategic goals and broad policy measures contained in the NCS do not, however, lend themselves easily to the formulation of programmes and projects for implementation. Therefore, preparation of an Action Plan has been initiated to provide the means of translating the strategy into policies, programmes and projects. This will be achieved through:

- defining in specific terms, and on the basis of the nation's environment and conservation policies, the strategic measures of the NCS that should affect policy formulation and implementation in the rest of the government; and
- articulating and describing integrated multi-sectoral conservation and development programmes and projects (IMCDP).

The Action Plan will also include a monitoring system through a carefully designed environmental management information system. As part of the National Development Programme (NDP) process, the NCS will be subject to regular reviews and updates.

## 4 Strategy Framework

The strategy framework consists of four different types of measures, including:

- the provision of the economic incentives required to stimulate sustainable development and to discourage over-utilization of natural resources;
- the enforcement of existing laws and regulations and, where appropriate, the introduction of new legislation;
- the improvement of planning and administrative procedures which require that full recognition is given to ecological needs through the definition of resource use zones; and
- the expansion of facilities directed to improving environmental education, training and research activities, as well as to raising public awareness about environmental issues.

## 5 Relationship to Planning and Decision-Making

Subsequent to the approval of the NCS document in 1990, the government set up an Advisory Board and an NCS (Coordinating) Agency with a mandate to further redefine and implement the NCS. Both institutions are currently part of the government and are located in the Ministry of Local Government, Lands and Housing. The Board is chaired by the Minister of Local Government, Lands and Housing.

The Board is serviced by the NCS (Coordinating) Agency which coordinates the execution of the Board's decisions and liaises with other organizations to ensure that the NCS goals and objectives are achieved through their integration with the work of the sectoral ministries and other interest groups throughout Botswana.

The institutional linkages between the Agency on the one hand and the central and local government on the other are operationalized through the appointment of Environmental Liaison Officers (ELOs) who are responsible for ensuring that their organizations comply with the strategic requirements of the NCS.

These institutional linkages are the main means by which coordination and implementation of the NCS are achieved. By providing an extensive consultative framework, they are also the means by which links with the national development planning process are operationalized. In addition, the National Development Programme has mandatory requirements for all sectoral ministries, departments, local authorities, parastatals and so on to show due regard for conservation and enhancement of the environment in the course of their work, in the interest of achieving sustainable development.

Further recommendations for an appropriate institutional framework have recently been made, which should foster a strategic functional relationship between the issues of macro-economic development planning coordinated by the Ministry of Finance and Development Planning, and those of conservation, coordinated by the NCS Board/Agency.

In this context, the NCS Board is mandated to give advice, coordinate, monitor, support and cooperate with the sectorally-organized ministries and local authorities in addressing natural resource concerns. The NCS Board and Agency do, however, take full responsibility for the activities that do not fall under the mandate of any sectoral ministry. These are currently being implemented under the three divisions which have been created for administrative convenience, namely:

a) policy programmes and projects;
b) environmental education and research; and
c) waste management.

Specific programmes and project activities currently being implemented by the NCS Board and Agency include the following.

*Environmental Impact Assessment Legislation*

The process of promulgating environmental impact assessment (EIA) legislation was initiated at the end of 1992 when the main principles of the proposed legislation were discussed and agreed. The EIA legislation will make it mandatory for development policies, programmes and projects of a given magnitude to be accompanied by professionally prepared and approved EIAs. The drafting instructions are currently being finalized for submission to the relevant government authorities.

*State of the Environmental Review*

The NCS mandates its Agency to prepare and publish a *State of the Environment Review* on a biennial basis. Preparation of the first of these has been initiated. The Review will reflect trends in the state of Botswana's natural resources and their use, and provide baseline data for an integrated resource monitoring system that should foster the process of sustainable development. The first Review will be completed and published by the first quarter of 1996.

*Ratification of the Convention on
Biological Diversity*

Botswana is in the process of ratifying the
Convention on Biological Diversity. This
will enable the country to qualify for the
requisite financial and other resources
needed to implement the aspects of the
NCS that underpin conservation of
biodiversity at the genetic, species and
ecosystems levels; sustainable use of
resources; and fair and equitable sharing
of benefits derived from the use of genetic
resources.

## 6 Lessons Learned

*Strengths of the Strategy*

The main strengths of the Botswana NCS
process have been that:

- it involved a comprehensive review of
  the legislative framework which
  revealed that substantive changes are
  required to improve the country's
  environmental laws;
- NCS institutions are obligated to
  prepare regular state of the
  environment reports;
- the NCS Act will provide the necessary
  powers to require planning and other
  authorities to prepare conservation and
  resource strategies at district level;
- the Act will also require the sectoral
  ministries to work closely with the

NCS Agency in discharging their
environmental responsibilities; and

- the strategy advocates the use of
  education and persuasion rather than
  penalties for environmental offences.
  (In particular, the strategy encourages
  the use of fiscal incentives and
  disincentives which discourage the
  abuse of the environment. For example,
  the strategy proposes the use of price
  incentives to improve rangeland
  management. This is a positive
  departure from the traditional heavy
  reliance on legislation.)

*Weaknesses of the Strategy*

The main weaknesses of the Botswana
NCS process include the facts that:

- the preparation of the NCS was
  undertaken when there were
  insufficient local skills and personnel to
  facilitate the process;
- there was an inadequate institutional
  framework and a lack of clearly defined
  authority. The institutional
  shortcomings of the current location
  within the Ministry of Local
  Government, Lands and Housing,
  which has line functions, lead to gaps in
  environmental policy formulation;
  inadequate integration of management;
  inadequate monitoring capacity;
  inadequate coordination; lack of
  capacity to resolve differences; and
  inadequate response capacity; and

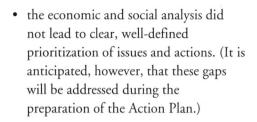

- the economic and social analysis did not lead to clear, well-defined prioritization of issues and actions. (It is anticipated, however, that these gaps will be addressed during the preparation of the Action Plan.)

*Overall Lessons*

Generally, it can be concluded that:

- promoting greater public awareness of environmental issues in particular and, more generally, of the concept of sustainable development is crucial to the success of preparing and implementing the NCS;
- without clear legislation and capable institutions, well-conceived policies and actions can not be translated into practice. A legal framework is needed to support structures for environmental management as well as to clarify their mandate and powers, and to define the structures' relations with other sectors of the government and civil society. An ideal and appropriate institutional location of the NCS Board and its Agency in government is crucial for the long-term success of the strategy;
- environmental problems are cross-sectoral and strategic environmental management therefore involves extensive cooperation with other sectoral ministries;
- training and capacity-building are essential, particularly in the early stages, in order to develop a critical mass of expertise.

| 7 | *Chronology* |
|---|---|
| 1983 | Botswana Government recognizes the need for preparation of an NCS. |
| 1984 | Preparation of the NCS begins. |
| 1990 | NCS adopted by Parliament as Government Paper No 2, 'National Policy on Natural Resources Conservation and Development'. |
| 1990 | NCS (Coordinating) Agency established, with an Advisory Board, both located in Ministry of Local Government, Lands and Housing. |

# *Eritrea*

*National Environmental
Management Plan*

NAIGZY GEBREMEDHIN, ERITREAN
AGENCY FOR THE ENVIRONMENT; AND
HAGOS YOHANNES, ERITREAN AGENCY
FOR THE ENVIRONMENT

**Estimated population 1993:** 3.5 million;
**Land area:** 120,000 km²; **Ecological
zones:** narrow Red Sea coastal plain,
central and northern highlands and
northwestern and southwestern lowlands;
**Climate:** arid and semi-arid; **Annual
rainfall:** 500–700 mm (200mm in coastal
desert zone); **Forest and woodland area:**
53,000 ha; **Main industries:** agriculture,
manufacturing (textiles) and minerals;
**Population growth rate** (1992–2000):
2.6 per cent

## 1 Introduction

As part of the process of establishing a new state, Eritrea has recently developed a National Environmental Management Plan for Eritrea (NEMP-E). This was produced in less than six months, through the coordinated efforts of staff from several ministries under the direction of the Ministerial Council on the Environment. The plan has been produced primarily with domestic financial and personnel resources in line with the country's development philosophy of self reliance. A grant of US$150,000 was obtained from the Heinrich Boll Foundation, and some support from the World Bank was provided for the field consultations.

The plan represents the framework within which phased actions will be implemented to enable national capacity-building for environmental management up to the year 2000 and beyond. The NEMP-E is a model plan in that its priorities were reached by a consensus of the people, government experts and acadaemia. Substantial inputs from the people of Eritrea were sought in the preparation of the NEMP-E.

The experience of Eritrea highlights a number of key issues concerning the development of environmental strategies or management plans. These include the importance of having a clear vision of what sustainable development means for the society in question, the extent to which foreign resources are needed, and the advantages and disadvantages of relying solely on domestic resources. In addition questions are raised about the extent to which the momentum and cooperation developed in the short period of strategy formulation can be maintained into the implementation phase, and the degree to which a rapid consultation process can ensure that the strategy is firmly rooted and supported by commu–nities once implementation begins. A further issue is the way in which esta–blished government departments will respond to a new coordinating body for environmental matters when their specific areas of interest and responsibility are affected.

## 2 Initiation of the Strategy

The need for a NEMP was recognized in the macro-economic policy document which was produced by the government of Eritrea in April 1994. This was less than three years after Eritrea achieved independence, following the 30-year liberation struggle. The macro-economic policy recognizes that environmental sustainability is an essential basis for achieving the development goals of the country, especially the alleviation of poverty. It notes the need for sound environmental management given the

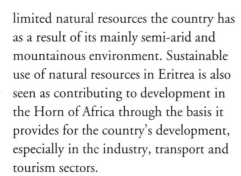

limited natural resources the country has as a result of its mainly semi-arid and mountainous environment. Sustainable use of natural resources in Eritrea is also seen as contributing to development in the Horn of Africa through the basis it provides for the country's development, especially in the industry, transport and tourism sectors.

The NEMP-E was prepared at the same time as many National Environmental Action Plans (NEAPs). Many NEAPS were prepared in Africa as a requirement for the World Bank's International Development Association (IDA) 10 funds. The NEMP-E was prepared solely as a result of domestic initiative, since Eritrea did not plan to seek loans from the World Bank and hence was not concerned about the requirements for access to IDA funds.

## 3 Development of the Strategy

The production of the NEMP-E involved five major steps:

- the establishment of a technical committee under the guidance of the Ministerial Council on the Environment;
- the development by the technical committee of a vision of what sustainable development should be for Eritrea;

- the identification of the main issues which need to be addressed;
- the collection of information on these main issues, including consultation with the public; and
- the drafting of the strategy.

About one-quarter of the time was spent on developing the vision and one-third on undertaking the consultation workshops, while the remainder of the time was spent on drafting.

In June 1994 a seven-member Ministerial Council on the Environment was appointed and by September of that year the technical committee had been established to undertake the strategy formulation. The committee comprised 14 persons drawn from several ministries.

The first task of the committee was to develop a clear vision of sustainable development for Eritrea. The technical committee identified five major elements:

- peace and the ability to resolve all types of conflicts through peaceful means;
- equity and egalitarianism;
- a change in the way the environment is perceived so that fatalistic views are replaced by a recognition of the role and potential of human action;
- meeting of the basic needs of the current population so that the interests of future generations can be considered and protected; and

- self-reliance, involving the belief that the country should not turn to external sources for support when there are domestic resources which can be used.

While the vision of sustainable development was developed by the technical committee, the main players in the formulation of the strategy were the public, who were consulted throughout the country in a series of workshops aiming to build a consensus on environmental priorities. A total of 23 meetings were held at different locations over a period of two months, involving consultation with over 3,000 people. The meetings lasted half a day and involved two separate gatherings at each location: first, representatives of the government departments, such as civil servants and extension workers; and second, leading members of the *baitos*, or village councils, who were selected by the Ministry of Local Government, as well as representatives of religious groups, NGOs, commercial organizations, and other interested parties. The purpose of having separate meetings was to ensure that the community leaders would be completely free to make their views known and would not feel inhibited by the presence of the government officials.

In the workshops, members of the Technical Team introduced six major subjects which they felt were of most pressing concern. For each of these a presentation was made identifying basic facts and important trends. The six subjects were:

- terrestrial systems;
- marine system;
- urban and built environment;
- human health and pollution;
- institutions and training; and
- major groups.

The presentations were carefully prepared at the appropriate level for the community. In addition, for each of the four different eco-geographical regions of the country the presentations were adjusted so that they were appropriate to the conditions with which people were familiar. After the presentations, the participants were invited to make comments about the nature of the problems in their area under these subject headings and to identify ways in which they could begin to address these problems.

The priorities raised by communities in these discussions included health, water and food, and these have been reflected in the priority programmes which have been developed in the NEMP-E (see Table 1 and Annex 1 for further details). The community priorities served to confirm those which were identified by the technical committee staff in their deliberations.

Following the consultations, the NEMP-E was drafted by the six task forces of the technical committee. The technical committee met twice weekly for a period of six weeks in order to ensure close coordination during the drafting of the Management Plan.

The Plan was produced in less than six months, a very short time for such an important strategic document. The reasons for this were partly due to the wish to respond quickly to the identified need for such a plan in the macro-economic policy document. Secondly, having made the original commitment to produce the NEMP-E in a specific time frame, it was not seen as acceptable to extend the time period even though additional consultations were required beyond those originally planned. In addition, the time frame could not be extended because the staff involved in the NEMP-E also had responsibilities to contribute to other processes, such as the biodiversity and anti-desertification strategies, and so had no choice but to complete the NEMP-E in the original time envisaged.

## 4 Finalizing and Publicizing the Plan

Once the draft NEMP-E had been prepared, a number of activities were arranged both to raise the profile of the plan and to ensure that the document had included the major views expressed by the communities. These activities started with a national conference, held 2–4 February 1995, at which 500 delegates, two-thirds of whom were members of the public, discussed the draft NEMP-E.

The purpose of this meeting was partly to confirm that the plan accurately reflected the views of the people the technical committee had consulted. In addition, it provided an opportunity for the delegates to comment further on the proposals in the plan. The participants recommended a change in the location of the Eritrean Agency for the Environment (EAE) from the technical committee's original recommendation (in the Office of the President) to within the Ministry of Local Government. Participants felt that the Ministry has the highest degree of contact with people. In addition, the participants requested that much more emphasis be placed on the need for further training and information dissemination to the public.

An international conference for government officials, invited donors and foreign organizations was held 8–9 February 1995, with 400 participants. This sought to show to the international community the concern which Eritrea has for environmental issues and to direct donors to particular areas for development support (for these two conferences the draft

NEMP-E was produced in three different languages: Tigrynia, Arabic and English).

A 'Green Week' was held between these two conferences with the objective of raising awareness on environmental issues. This involved a number of activities, including:

- a school children's convention on the Eritrean environment;
- special church and mosque sermons considering the environment;
- films and displays at various public places;
- a clean-up campaign; and
- a car-free day.

Feedback from all these activities was included in finalizing the NEMP-E. In addition, comments were received on the draft NEMP-E from 20 ministries, the World Bank, UNEP, IUCN and some international NGOs, and these were incorporated into the final document.

## 5 Specific Recommendations

Eritrea's NEMP views the terrestrial, coastal and human environments as a triangle of interconnected use and exploitation. The status and fate of all three domains are strongly influenced by national macro-economic policies. Hence, the NEMP-E has been developed to help integrate issues of environmental sustainability with macro-economic and other national development policies. It has been accepted as a Sustainable Development Strategy by the United Nations Development Programme (UNDP).

With this broad approach, the government sees the NEMP-E as a sustainable development strategy which has a special emphasis on the environment. The Plan has some elements which go beyond its national border with discussions of marine issues in the Red Sea and grazing issues in nomadic lowlands, both of which are of regional significance.

The most critical component of the NEMP-E is the establishment of the EAE. The Ministerial Council on the Environment, which was largely responsible for the development the NEMP-E, will be expanded beyond its present membership (the Ministries of Agriculture, Construction, Energy, Mines and Water Resources, Health, Trade and Industry, Local Government and Marine Resources) to include representatives of NGOs, the Chamber of Commerce, private industry and commerce, and Asmara University.

The powers and responsibilities of the EAE, the Head of EAE, and the Environmental Council will be defined and elaborated in the Eritrean Environment Act, to be developed in the first programme phase of the NEMP-E.

Particular points of emphasis in the NEMP-E are:

- a call for an interdisciplinary rather than sectoral approach to research and management, emphasizing that the greatest national benefits will result from an integration of NEMP-E guidelines and national macro-economic policies;
- recognition of the need to maintain the vitality and diversity of environmental systems, with emphasis on the NEMP-E's role in optimizing rather than maximizing resource use;
- emphasis on the role of local people as the day-to-day managers of natural resources, and their need to be involved in both planning and implementation to ensure equitable and effective development; and
- a dynamic view of planning and management, which are seen as activities which should involve all participants in monitoring and adapting to situations as they arise.

## 6 Implementation and Anticipated Results

There are a number of steps which now have to be followed to turn the NEMP-E from a document into an effective process for integrating environmental issues into Eritrea's development.

The first step is to prepare and pass the Eritrean Environment Act. This will establish the EAE which will be attached to the Ministry of Local Government and which will be a government agency. The powers of the Agency will be specified and will include responsibilities to coordinate the implementation of the NEMP-E and catalyse action in the environmental field.

The EAE will seek to encourage the development of environmental pro-grammes in population, monitoring, water, health, land management, forestry, human settlements, energy, national parks, coastal-zone management, industry and waste management, information, and group strengthening. In particular, em-phasis will be placed upon increasing the capacity of local people and institutions, through their involvement in planning and implementing programmes. Their attention will be especially directed to the priority areas which were identified in the consultation process. These include arresting land degradation and promoting sustainable agriculture, sustainable energy and water-source development, and improved environmental health and sanitation. The EAE will also be responsible for ensuring that government and private organizations consider the environmental impacts of their economic and development activities and protect the environment.

These initiatives will have to recognize the existing institutional situation, however. At present, guidance for commercial and business activities in Eritrea is provided by the Cabinet of Ministers of the State of Eritrea and the country's macro-economic policies. These policies, together with national legislation and international agreements, provide an overall national framework for development in Eritrea and help determine priorities for action. A number of ministries currently address environmental problems, but there is no coordinating mechanism to do so; a holistic approach to development and management has been missing. It is envisaged that linking the activities of these various ministries will be one of the many major challenges for the EAE.

While the powers of the Agency will be considerable in order to achieve effective influence over the line ministries, it may be necessary for it to appeal to the Ministerial Council on the Environment in the case of disagreements. To facilitate the EAE's activities with the ministries, contact people will be established in each ministry and will be responsible for helping to ensure that the environmental concerns of the Agency are kept on the agenda of each ministry.

In order to facilitate the achievement of the goals of the NEMP-E a number of programmes and project activities have been identified. These are summarized in Table 1, while more details are provided in Annex 1.

## Table 1. NEMP-E Implementation Needs

| Plan Sector | Institutional Requirements |
| --- | --- |
| Environmental law and institutions | EAE; Council of Ministers on the Environment; the Eritrean Environment Act |
| Interdisciplinary assessment of the environment; human population and critical resource interactions | EAE in cooperation with bilateral national partners |
| Environmental monitoring and assessment programme | EAE, Unit for Environmental Research |
| Water management programme; six priority programmes | Water Resources Department, Ministry of Mines, Energy and Water Resources |
| Pollution control and environmental health programme; five priority programmes | Department of Public Health to create new rural and urban sanitation unit |
| Land management programme; six priority programmes | Ministry of Agriculture; land and soil unit, soil and water conservation unit, rangeland management unit and land commission |
| Forest management programme; five priority programmes | Ministry of Agriculture; Forestry Department |
| Human settlements management programme; five priority programmes | Ministry of Construction, formulation of national shelter strategy; institutional arrangements to follow including creating new unit |
| Energy policy and conservation and mining programme; seven priority programmes | Ministry of Energy, Mines, and Water Resources |
| National parks and wildlife conservation programme; four priority programmes | Institutional framework of the wildlife protection; Department of the Ministry of Agriculture |
| Integrated coastal-zone management programme; three priority programmes | Ministry of Marine Resources; permanent committee on oil spill contingencies to be established |
| Industry, environment and waste management programme; three priority programmes | Ministry of Trade and Industry; creation of a new chemicals management unit |
| Environmental information education and training programme | Ministry of Education; creation of environmental education centre |
| Strengthening the role of major groups; three priority programmes | Ministry of Local Government; Eritrean Chamber of Commerce; creation of new unit and focal point |

| Personnel Requirements | Financial Requirements and Time Frame |
|---|---|
| EAE staff, expatriate staff may be seconded to EAE on bilateral agreements | US$3,500,000 (1996–1999); external, US$2,000,000 |
| Contracted consultant experts, supervision by EAE | US$350,000 (1996–1998); external US$300,000 |
| Contracted consultants/experts, supervision by EAE | US$350,000 (1996–1998); external US$300,000 |
| Hydrologists, meteorologists, civil engineers | US$8,870,000 (1995–1999); external US$8,100,000 |
| One expert each for public health, vector control and nutrition | US$2,066,000 (1995–2000); external US$1,700,000 |
| Experts | US$7,550,000 (1994–2000); external US$6,125,000 |
| Foresters, soil conservationists, sociologist and cartographer | US$20,900,000 (1995–2003); external US$14,400,000 |
| Housing experts, computer experts, civil engineers | US$3,820,000 (1995–2001); external US$2,950,000 |
| Energy and mining experts | US$8,610,000 (1993–1998); external US$7,350,000 |
| Conservation educators, botanists, wildlife ecologists, conservation biologists | US$1,750,000 (1995–2000); external US$740,000 |
| To be provided by Ministry of Marine Resources | US$7,700,000 (1995–1998); external US$6,500,000 |
| Chemist/toxicologist, information expert | US$900,000 (1995–1998); external US$700,000 |
| Environmental education and training expert | US$405,000 (1996–1998); external US$305,000 |
| Public administration expert, environmentalist | US$2,600,000 (1995–1998); external US$1,950,000 |

## 7 Issues

### Need for a Vision and Self-reliance

The key characteristic of the Eritrean NEMP is that it is based on a clear vision of what sustainable development means for the country. This vision has been developed over 30 years of warfare and struggle for independence. Through this experience a common consensus about sustainable development is seen to exist within the society. Central to this consensus is the principle of self-reliance, which has been the basis of preparation for the NEMP-E. There have been no donor inputs to the NEMP and the work being undertaken is done totally by local staff and the communities. Also of note is the way in which the *baito* system has provided a mechanism for communities to be represented in the regional workshops.

### Differing Perceptions

A number of problems have been identified in the process of developing the plan and initiating implementation. The most important problem is the differences in perception between the public and the technical committee concerning the priority issues in environmental management. Although the general areas of priority were similar, the public focused on meeting immediate needs while the technical committee took a more long-term ecological view.

In addition, despite the widespread participation of communities in the struggle for independence, there remains a belief among the public that, now that peace has been achieved, development problems – including environmental ones – will be solved by the government.

A final issue is the extent to which donors will respond favourably to requests for funding elements of the NEMP-E when they have not been involved in the development of the document.

### Implementation Concerns

**Ability to coordinate:** The development of an independent EAE is envisaged, with the power to coordinate and monitor the activities of different government agencies and the private sector. There are some doubts, however, about the extent to which it will be able to fulfil its coordinating role. This is despite the fact that during the preparation of the plan new dimensions of interministerial cooperation and cohesion were established based on a common concern for the environment and a recognition that environmental protection requires a strong partnership between people and government.

There has already been an indication that the consensus among ministries involved in the preparation of the NEMP-E is falling apart as progress towards implementation and the establishment of the EAE is made. Hence it seems likely that the EAE will require major political support if it is to be effective. This will be provided primarily by the Minister of Local Government, who is also the Vice-President, and to whom this Agency will report, although the practical aspects of this support for the EAE are yet to be worked out.

**Community ownership:** The final concern is the extent to which the plan is firmly rooted in the communities and owned by them. The regional workshops were brief because of the time frame and because the involvement of communities was naturally limited. However, considerable efforts have been made to ensure increased and long-term participation by communities in the implementation of the NEMP-E. These include the establishment of the Eritrean People's Forum on the Environment and an Eritrean Environment Fund which will be administered by the Forum. The Forum will consist of representatives from the local *baitos*, who will regularly review the environmental issues identified in the NEMP-E and the progress made in addressing them. In addition, each community will be asked to adopt an environmental agenda for sustainable development through its *baito*. Specific activities on these agendas will be funded, thereby facilitating the implementation of the NEMP-E. In this way the level of community involvement in the prepa-ration of the NEMP-E will be developed further and local ownership of the plan will be strengthened.

| 8 | *Chronology* |
|---|---|
| 1994 | April: Need for a National Environment Management Plan recognized in the macro-economic policy document. |
| | June: Ministerial Council on the Environment appointed. |
| | September: Technical committee established to undertake the strategy formulation. |
| | September to October: Consultation meetings held at 23 different locations. |
| 1995 | December to January 1995: Drafting of NEMP-E by six task forces and the technical committee. |
| | 2–9 February: 'Green Week' of activities to raise awareness about environmental issues. |
| | 2–4 February: National Conference on NEMP-E. |
| | 8–9 February: International Conference on NEMP-E. |

## *Annex 1. NEMP-E: Envisaged Programme of Activities*

*Environmental Law, Institution and International Cooperation Programme*

- establishment of the Eritrean Agency for the Environment (EAE)
- EAGER: Environmental Assessment Guidelines for Eritrea
- capacity-building to promote environmental security and conflict management

*Interdisciplinary Assessment of the Eritrean Environment: Human Population and Critical Resources Interactions*

*Establishment of Environmental Monitoring and Assessment Network*

*Water Management Programme: Six Priority Programmes*

- water development master plan
- establishment of national hydrological network (priority 2)
- groundwater resources inventory
- preparation of water law
- establishment of a national climatological network
- water conservation measures

*Human Health and Environmental Issues: Five Priority Programmes*

- demonstration of ventilated improved pit latrines
- environmentally sound malaria control
- schistosomiasis situation analysis: towards development of schistosomiasis control
- leishmaniasis survey
- eradication of iodine deficiency disorders (IDD) in Eritrea

*Land Management Programme: Six Priority Programmes*

- preparation and application of environmental guidelines for land classification
- supporting national information centre on natural resources
- land development master plan
- supporting soil and water conservation research
- soil fertility conservation: environmentally sound agriculture through eco-farming
- the improvement of rangelands management.

*Forest Management Programme: Five Priority Programmes*

- fuelwood plantation development
- afforestation and soil conservation on highly degraded catchments
- permanent forest woodland closure
- social forestry development
- agro-forestry research development, model farmers pilot project

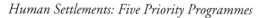

*Human Settlements: Five Priority Programmes*

- formulation of a national shelter strategy
- low-cost sanitation for solid waste and sewage systems in Asmara and Massawa
- information, training and data management
- feasibility study to develop site and service scheme in five cities
- manual for sustainable urban planning and management

*Energy Policy and Conservation and Mining Programme*

- comprehensive energy survey
- promotion of renewable energy in remote rural areas
- alternative energy for lime and brick manufacturing: pilot demonstration project
- LPG storage depot, Massawa
- assessment and mitigation of mercury poisoning in gold-mining process
- strengthening the institutional capacity of the Department of Mines Control
- rehabilitation of Assab refinery

*National Parks and Wildlife Conservation Programme*

- conservation education
- survey of elephant and wild ass populations
- Gash Setit and Buri Peninsula national parks, botanical garden, animal orphanage
- protection of biological diversity

*Integrated Coastal Management Programme*

- development and implementation of an integrated coastal zone management plan
- baseline information on coral reef areas that may be developed for tourism
- development of coastal and marine protected area systems for Eritrea

*Industry and Environment and Waste Management Programme: Three Priority Programmes*

- first phase of non-waste and low-waste technology (NLWT), database on NLWT
- building Eritrea's capacity to manage chemicals: legislation and management
- recycling of waste water from textile industry

*Environmental Information, Education and Training Programme*

*Strengthening the Role of Major Groups: Three Priority Programmes*

- strengthening local administration in environmental protection
- expanding the role of major groups in promoting sustainable development
- strengthening role of NGOs and chamber of commerce in environmental protection and enhancement

# *Ethiopia*

## *National Conservation Strategy*

Kifle Lemma, Ministry of Natural Resources and Environmental Protection; Setargew Demilew, Ministry of Planning and Economic Development; and Tewolde Berhan G Egziabher, Ministry of Natural Resources and Environmental Protection

**Estimated population 1992:** 50.3 million; **Land area:** 1,101,000 km$^2$; **Ecological zones:** extensive lowlands with two highland massifs, separated by the Rift Valley; **Climate:** tropical, distinct wet season; **Annual rainfall:** 500–2,200 mm; **Forest and woodland area:** 268,700 km$^2$; **GNP per capita:** US$110; **Main industries:** agriculture, especially subsistence farming; **ODA received per capita:** US$23.30; **Population growth rate (1992–2000):** 3 per cent; **Life expectancy at birth:** 47.5 years; **Adult literacy rate:** 32.7 per cent; **Access to safe water:** 25 per cent; **Access to health services:** 46 per cent; **Access to sanitation:** 19 per cent

## 1 Introduction

Ethiopia is one of the countries facing serious ecological imbalances. During this century natural resource degradation has accelerated and a destructive cycle of land use has developed in parts of the country involving deforestation followed by continuous cropping and grazing with little or no investment in the soil. This provides few opportunities for the natural vegetation to regenerate, reduces the productivity of the soil leaving it susceptible to erosion, and affects the hydrological cycle thereby altering the regimes of the rivers. Drought is also a recurrent feature in the country and soil degradation has increased the impact of this problem upon crops.

The present methods of using natural resources in Ethiopia are causing their depletion at a rate which is accelerating. However, despite these problems, there is no doubt that Ethiopia as a whole has an adequate resource base to support its present population at rising, rather than falling, standards of living provided appropriate natural resource management practices are developed. The challenge today, which the National Conservation Strategy (NCS) must help the country face, is to develop these improved management practices for the sustained use of natural resources and identify the circumstances which will facilitate their adoption.

The NCS takes a holistic view of the country's natural, human-made and cultural resources and their use and abuse. It seeks to integrate existing and future federal and regional government planning in all sectors that impinge on the natural and human-made environments. The purpose of the NCS project is the assessment of the status and trends in the use and management of the resource base of Ethiopia, the formulation of a policy and strategy framework which addresses the key issues which have been identified, and the development of a National Action Plan and Investment Programme, including legislative measures and management and operational arrangements, for implementation. The formulation process has been country-wide, multi-sectoral and participatory and implementation will be decentralized through the new regional structure.

The Ethiopian NCS was initiated in 1989 by the Office of the National Committee for Central Planning (ONCCP) following contacts with The World Conservation Union (IUCN) about land-use planning and natural resource management. ONCCP subsequently became the Ministry of Planning and Economic Development (MOPED) and is now the Ministry of Economic Development and Cooperation (MEDAC).

The first project agreement was signed by the Ethiopian government and IUCN on

15 March 1990 for help in drafting an NCS from May 1990 to April 1992. The formulation phase was formally launched at the National Conference held in Addis Ababa in May 1990. Following the conference a Secretariat was established in ONCCP. When the Ministry of Natural Resources, Development and Environmental Protection was created, the Secretariat moved to the new Ministry, and it is now located in the National Environmental Protection Authority (NEPA).

## 2 Phase One: Commencement

After the decision was taken by the Ethiopian government to develop an NCS, IUCN was requested to advise and assist in the work. The first phase in this process was the development of an overview status report.

This report provided a summary review of the environmental situation in Ethiopia in the late 1980s. It was based on extensive discussions with government officials, donor representatives and NGOs and a number of private individuals, as well as a thorough reading of recent literature on the country's development situation. The report also formed the basis for discussions about how the NCS should proceed.

Phase One of the NCS (1989–90) process focused on the identification of key environment and development issues and

the formulation of a conceptual framework for the NCS. The process also involved an assessment of the institutional arrangements which affect environmental and natural resource management.

## 3 Scope and Objectives

The main issues addressed by the strategy are either sectoral or cross-sectoral.

*Sectoral Issues*

The sectoral issues which the NCS has addressed included:

- forestry conservation and development;
- soil and water conservation and land husbandry;
- water resources;
- mineral resources;
- energy resources;
- cultural heritage;
- biological diversity;
- rangelands and pastoral development;
- human settlements, urban environment and environmental health;
- control and management of industrial waste, hazardous materials and pollution; and
- air pollution and climate change.

*Cross-Sectoral Issues*

The cross-sectoral issues addressed through the NCS have included:

- population and resources;
- people's participation in natural resource management;
- tenure and access rights;
- national and regional land-use plans;
- social, cultural and gender issues;
- environmental economics;
- environmental information systems;
- environmental research;
- science and technology;
- environmental impact assessment (EIA); and
- environmental education.

*Components of the Strategy*

The NCS document has three components. The first is a comprehensive review of the *Status and Trends in the Use and Management of Ethiopia's Natural Resources, Human-Made Environment and its Cultural Heritage.* This is based on the stock-taking and surveys undertaken at the local, zonal, regional and national levels. This review identifies the trends in resource use and their environmental, economic and socio-cultural implications.

The second component is the *National Policy Framework for the Sustainable Development and Management of Ethiopia's Natural, Human-Made and Cultural Resources and Environment.* This sets out the objectives, guiding principles and key strategies for the 11 cross-sectoral areas and sectors, and the institutional legislative framework for implementation.

It is based on the regional consultations, workshops and conferences undertaken under the auspices of the Ethiopian Forestry Action Programme and the National Country Programme planning process of the Transitional Government, as well as a number of new national policy documents.

The third component is an integrated and prioritized *National Action Plan and Investment Programme for the Sustainable Development and Management of Ethiopia's Natural, Human-made and Cultural Resources and Environment.* This will take its final shape upon completion of the Regional Conservation Strategies (RCSs), and will detail an integrated set of programmes, projects and actions, institutional structures and operational procedures for the implementation of the NCS.

## 4 Phase Two: Formulation

Phase Two of the NCS process (1990–94) focused on the development of a policy and institutional framework and action plan for the NCS. This was undertaken by the NCS Secretariat which was established in December 1990 and consisted of a director, two experts and an IUCN technical advisor. Their work involved a detailed analysis of the issues raised at the NCS Conference with extensive national, sub-national and local consultations involving consideration of sectoral and cross-sectoral policies. The role of the Secretariat was to facilitate cross-sectoral and interministerial discussions.

The NCS formulation process was undertaken on three fronts:

a) the formulation of RCSs, action plans and investment programmes, which is still ongoing;
b) the formulation of national sectoral policies, strategies, actions plans and tentative investment programmes; and
c) the formulation of cross-sectoral strategies and an institutional and legal framework.

*Regional Consultations and Strategy Formulation*

In 1992, the then Transitional Government of Ethiopia (TGE) announced a radical restructuring of the country's administration with the formation of 14 autonomous regions, which are sub-divided into zones. Five regions subsequently joined together reducing the numbers of regions to ten. This restructuring of government required a radical change in the NCS formulation process as the need to formulate RCSs was recognized in order for the national strategy to be implemented, given the federal government structure that was emerging. To provide assistance to the enlarged regional strategy development programme, a separate agreement was

signed between the TGE and the United Nations Sudano–Sahelian Office (UNSO) to run that programme from May 1991 to April 1994.

The regional/zonal process has moved forward in four stages. The job was, and is, being performed by regional/zonal task forces with the guidance of experts in the NCS Secretariat. During the first stage the NCS staff, ie the director, the technical advisor and the two technical experts, visited regions and zones to give assistance and guidance on how to collect data and how to analyze and synthesize the information obtained.

Assessment questions were prepared by the NCS Secretariat and distributed to all the regional/zonal task forces. The questions were intended as an aid to developing a method of assessment. Through field trips the NCS Secretariat experts explained the assessment questions to the concerned professionals in the regions and zones. The task forces were not limited by the assessment questions; they developed and applied them according to their specific situations. The task forces consulted with central and local government officials, NGO field workers, and individual farmers, elders, religious leaders, women and extension workers. All these helped them to know how natural resources were managed by various communities, the state of the ecosystems, and the problems and key environmental issues of their respective zones and regions.

The initial stock-taking and assessment of resources and consultations at the village and *wereda* (sub-zonal) levels, usually on a sample basis, were carried out in the 28 regions which had existed before the fall of the previous government. Many of these former regions are now zones in the new regions but the reports were written about the old regions. As a result a few new regions have required additional information and assessment for small areas now under their jurisdiction since they feel that previously they were not covered satisfactorily.

During the second stage the key resource issues, problems and potential were identified at the zonal level, leading to the preparation of a framework for a sustainable development strategy. Again, as a result of the additional assessment in some of the new regions the identifications so far made may need to be adjusted.

The third stage will be the holding of regional conferences in all the regions where a draft RCS will be considered.

During the fourth stage, regional action plans and investment programmes will be developed and subsequent to that the National Action Plan and Investment Programme will take its final shape. The National Policy and Strategy Framework

and the Regional Strategy Report will be used for this purpose.

The initial survey stage started in late 1991 when the country still comprised 28 regions. Interministerial task forces were established in all of the former 28 regions with the regional office (now Bureau) of the ONCCP being the focal agency. The NCS Secretariat provided guidelines but emphasized that, given the extremely varied conditions in the country, they were to be used in a very flexible way. Notwithstanding the difficult conditions in some parts of the country at the time, and despite the lack of transportation and equipment, many regions were able to complete the first stage before the regional reorganization took place in late 1992 following the change of government.

Fortunately many of the old regions became zones during the regional reorganization. As a result, most of the old regional task forces have become zonal task forces, although in most cases there was an almost complete turnover of personnel. However, the documentation remained to provide the basis for the second stage. In some cases, where the old regions were divided in more than one zone, it was necessary to establish new zonal task forces. As a result the number of task forces rose from 28 to 40.

With the administrative reorganization, in which elected regional governments took over administrative authority, it was considered necessary to provide regional rather than national coordination and policy guidance to the regional, zonal and local level consultation and formulation process. To this end, Conservation Strategy Steering Committees were established at the regional government level. These regional committees include:

- the elected vice president for economic development;
- the heads of the Bureau of Planning and Economic Development, Agriculture (which now includes Natural Resources Development and Environmental Protection), and Water Development; and
- a senior representative of the Regional Development Association NGO.

From these committees the Regional Environmental Coordinating Committees have now been developed.

Progress with the preparation of the RCS is continuing and the regional conference to discuss the draft strategy has been held in one region, with five more expected in the near future. The other regions are still drafting their RCSs; they will arrange their conferences once the strategies are complete.

The last stage of the process, the development of detailed regional action plans and investment programmes, was

started after April 1994 and was expected to take about 18 months to complete. This will involve a detailed consideration of the priorities and strategies agreed to at the regional conferences, and in the National Policy Framework and the National Action Plan and Investment Programme of late 1994.

*National Sectoral and Cross-Sectoral Strategy Formulation*

Ethiopia's development is managed through six programme areas in the Country Development Programme. The 11 sectoral strategies, which have been developed under the auspices of the NCS, contribute to programmes 1, 2 and 4 of the Country Development Programme. There is also a close link with the Ethiopian Forestry Action Programme. The NCS sectoral policy formulation was generally undertaken using the sectoral line ministries and agencies as focal points.

The 11 cross-sectoral policy and strategy areas have been identified and developed as part of ongoing strategic planning. Other macro national policy formulation activities taking place in various relevant government agencies have also been taken into consideration.

*Second National NCS Conference*

The written outputs of the second phase of the NCS process were reviewed at the

Second National NCS Conference in May 1994. The Conference was attended by representatives from all regions, national government institutions, donors and NGOs. Participants provided comments and amendments which were incorporated in the final version of the documents. The feedback from the Second National Conference and the Interministerial Committee's amendments, the policy framework, institutional arrangements, action plan and compilation of investment programmes were included in the submission to the Council of Ministers.

## 5 Relationship to Development Planning

The NCS Secretariat, based in NEPA, works jointly with a recently established Environmental Planning Unit (EPU) in MEDAC to support the development and implementation of the RCSs. The EPU provides training and support to the regional and zonal environmental coordinating committees (RECCs and ZECCs) which will provide cross-sectoral coordination of the formulation and implementation of the RCSs. The RECCs and ZECCs are composed of the representatives of the relevant line bureau at the appropriate level and will be responsible also for the integration of environmental considerations into development initiatives and plans which MEDAC coordinates at all levels.

In the implementation phase of the strategy the NCS Secretariat and the newly established EPU will perform the following activities:

- integrate the NCS throughout the Government of Ethiopia;
- strengthen the technical capacity of MEDAC;
- coordinate environmental inputs from other ministries into development planning activities;
- ensure that appropriate institutional linkages with other ministries and organizations, particularly NGOs, are developed to support the implementation of NCS at all levels and in all sectors;
- train members of MEDAC, the RECCs, and others in environmental planning, environmental economics, project appraisal, monitoring and evaluation;
- provide guidelines to assist the regions in the formulation and implementation of strategic environmental plans; and
- coordinate all activities with the NCS Secretariat.

## 6 Strengths and Weaknesses in the Development Phase

### Operational Problems

A number of factors slowed the formulation of the NCS. These included:

- deterioration of security conditions in 1990/91 before the programme could be fully initiated;
- restructuring of the country's administrative regions, from 28 to 14 and subsequently to 10, with 40 zones;
- establishment of new zones in some regions requiring additional assessment;
- lack of qualified personnel at zonal and sometimes at regional levels;
- transfer of individual task force members at zonal levels and steering committee members at regional levels to the zones or regions;
- difficulties in establishing task forces at the zonal level due to the fact that members of task forces were from different bureaux;
- lack of offices and office equipment in almost all zones to finalize their field findings;
- communication problems with the zonal task force; and
- pressure from the World Bank to undertake an NEAP.

*Weaknesses in the Process*

A number of weaknesses can also be identified in the process, including:

- poor information dissemination;
- insufficient training for regional and zonal task forces; and
- slow progress at the decision-making level towards the adoption of the NCS document.

*Strengths*

A number of factors have facilitated the NCS formulation process. These include:

- strong political support for the formulation process;
- committed (although few) NCS Secretariat staff;
- breadth of the formulation process, with country-wide and multi-sectoral aspects following a holistic approach;
- focus on the underlying causes (and not just the symptoms);
- action orientation;
- donor involvement in the environmental investment programme; and
- participatory aspects.

*Training*

The NCS process has also involved a number of training activities which have been important in building up capacity. This has mainly involved the staff of the Secretariat who have made many field visits to the regions with guidelines for undertaking the RCSs. Mini-workshops in some regions on the topics of 'Strategies for Sustainability' and 'Participatory Rural Appraisal' have also been carried out. This is an ongoing activity which will be carried out in the rest of the regions which have not yet had these workshops. These regional workshops are the continuation of the 'Workshop on Regional/Local Strategy Development' held in Addis

Ababa between 5–8 June 1995, a national workshop run and sponsored by IUCN. In addition, one of the technical experts was sent to the UK for a Masters degree in Environment, Development and Policy. This strengthened the technical capacity of the NCS Secretariat.

## 7 Phase Three: Implementation

### Institutional Setting

Implementation will take place largely at the regional level. Therefore, support will be needed to strengthen the skills, capacity and institutions in the regions to ensure the implementation of environmental management projects and activities identified through the first two phases of the NCS process.

Concerning the operational arrangements for programme implementation, there will be two types of agencies which will make up the management structure of the National Policy on Natural Resources and the Environment: the coordinating agency (NEPA) and the implementing agencies (federal line ministries, regional bureaux, private organizations and communities). The coordinating agency has a primary responsibility for coordinating the implementation of all programme components in the National Policy on Natural Resources and the Environment. Programme components will be imple-

mented by specified implementing agencies who will take responsibility for day-to-day management and control. Implementing agencies may be found at any level of administration, from the central down to the local. This mechanism will replicate itself in more or less the same manner at regional, zonal and *wereda* levels.

### Integration and Harmonization

By integrating and harmonizing the different existing strategies, it is expected that the NCS will enhance the capacity and effectiveness of existing and subsequent strategies. In this respect the NCS will play an important role in coordinating sectoral strategies, which include the Food and Nutrition Strategy, the Soil Conservation Strategy, land-use policy and legislation, the Ethiopian Forestry Action Plan, the Disaster Prevention and Preparedness Strategy, the Agro-Ecological Zonation Study, and so on.

The difference between the Ethiopian NCS and an NEAP has been a question throughout the process. At the NCS conference in May 1990 there was considerable debate on the title to be used (NCS or NEAP). It was finally decided to retain the title of NCS for convenience, recognizing that it was the type and characteristics of the 'process' which was most important. The World Bank mission of 1994 was convinced that the Ethiopian

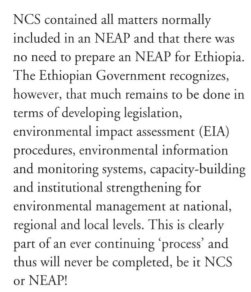

NCS contained all matters normally included in an NEAP and that there was no need to prepare an NEAP for Ethiopia. The Ethiopian Government recognizes, however, that much remains to be done in terms of developing legislation, environmental impact assessment (EIA) procedures, environmental information and monitoring systems, capacity-building and institutional strengthening for environmental management at national, regional and local levels. This is clearly part of an ever continuing 'process' and thus will never be completed, be it NCS or NEAP!

*Capacity Development*

Phase Three of the NCS project will seek to identify or establish appropriate institutions at regional level to implement the projects and activities described in the NCS document and to provide action-oriented training opportunities for national, regional and local staff.

Training will be provided to assist the RECCs in carrying out their duties effectively. To ensure that training opportunities are equitable across regions and sectors, the NCS Secretariat and EPU will coordinate the training and support for all RECCs. Similar committees will be established at the zonal level. Both committees will be responsible for coordinating the implementation of the NCS activities at regional and zonal levels.

Training and skills required by RECCs for the implementation phase are:

- integrated planning;
- environmental economics;
- computer use;
- environmental assessment;
- map reading;
- environmental law;
- communication skills; and
- PRA methodology.

In addition, the needs of particular regions will be assessed and additional training activities could be carried out in the future. In organizing and providing training courses, the EPU and NCS Secretariat will work together. They will also develop guidelines which will be tested and adapted for use at regional and zonal levels.

*The Communication Component*

Ethiopia is still, essentially, an oral society. This is not surprising given that the country lacks adequate infrastructure, ie roads, electricity, radio and television transmitters. In such a situation radio is likely to have the greatest reach. Similarly, where television exists, it is a more influential medium than the press.

The implementation phase envisages the following specific activities under the Communication Programme for the NCS as included in the third phase project:

- development of a communication strategy for Phase Three;
- edit and desktop-publish relevant NCS background reports;
- desktop-publish the Ethiopia NCS documents;
- prepare briefing kits on the NCS;
- networking, wall newspapers, and storytelling posters; and
- training in communication skills.

The Communication Programme will be carried out by the NCS Secretariat in partnership with concerned ministries, agencies, and NGOs. This will provide overall communications planning and guidance for NCS programmes at both national and regional levels, and training in the use of communication tools for a range of audiences.

*Monitoring and Assessment*

Currently there is no monitoring, evaluation and policy review system to cover all the cross-sectoral and sectoral areas in the National Policy on Natural Resources and the Environment. Effective implementation and appropriate timely adjustments will require feedback on the progress of implementation and the impact of policies, legislation, action plans and investment programmes. MEDAC and NEPA through EPU and the NCS Secretariat respectively, will establish and implement a system to regularly monitor and assess the effectiveness of the NCS

policy framework and action plans, and to review on an annual basis NCS principles, objectives and basic assumptions. The overall monitoring of all development policies and investment programmes including the NCS is the responsibility of MEDAC.

In the implementation phase of the NCS, strategies have been formulated for monitoring, evaluation and policy review to help find out whether the process is on the right track or not. The strategies are:

- develop internal environmental monitoring and evaluation systems, and train human resources to run them in all responsible line ministries;
- produce annual reports on the environment and development by MEDAC as well as by the ministry or authority responsible for environment;
- discuss the environmental situation in annual meetings of communities at the community level and annual meetings of environmental coordinating committees at successively higher levels up to the national level;
- MEDAC to receive presentations and submissions on environmental matters affecting communities, *weredas,* zones and regions from environmental coordinating committees at various levels; and
- prepare in the Prime Minister's Office annual reports to Parliament on environment and development.

37

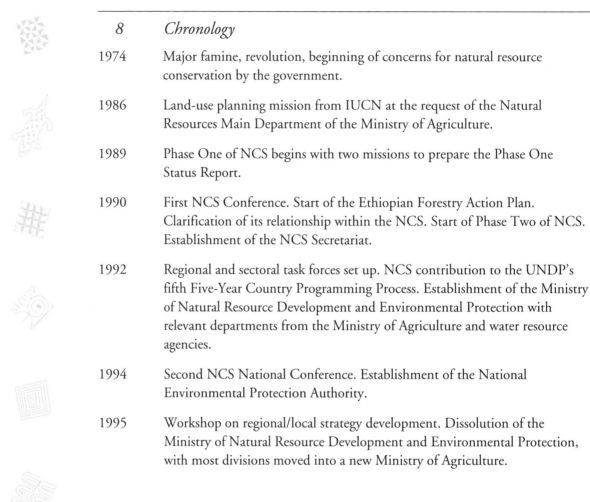

| 8 | *Chronology* |
|---|---|
| 1974 | Major famine, revolution, beginning of concerns for natural resource conservation by the government. |
| 1986 | Land-use planning mission from IUCN at the request of the Natural Resources Main Department of the Ministry of Agriculture. |
| 1989 | Phase One of NCS begins with two missions to prepare the Phase One Status Report. |
| 1990 | First NCS Conference. Start of the Ethiopian Forestry Action Plan. Clarification of its relationship within the NCS. Start of Phase Two of NCS. Establishment of the NCS Secretariat. |
| 1992 | Regional and sectoral task forces set up. NCS contribution to the UNDP's fifth Five-Year Country Programming Process. Establishment of the Ministry of Natural Resource Development and Environmental Protection with relevant departments from the Ministry of Agriculture and water resource agencies. |
| 1994 | Second NCS National Conference. Establishment of the National Environmental Protection Authority. |
| 1995 | Workshop on regional/local strategy development. Dissolution of the Ministry of Natural Resource Development and Environmental Protection, with most divisions moved into a new Ministry of Agriculture. |

# Guinea-Conakry

*National Environmental Action Plan*

HUBERT LEBLANC, FORMER TECHNICAL
ADVISOR TO THE GUINEA-CONAKRY
NEAP

**Estimated population 1992:** 6.1 million;
**Land area:** 246,000 km²; **Ecological
zones:** coast with mangrove forest, narrow
coastal plain, savannah plains in east,
forested highlands in south; **Climate:**
tropical with wet season from May to
October; **Annual rainfall:** 4923 mm (at
Conakry); **Forest and woodland area:**
144,700 km²; **GNP per capita:** US$490;
**Main industries:** agriculture, minerals;
**ODA received per capita:** US$66.60;
**Population growth rate** (1992–2000):
3.0 per cent; **Life expectancy at birth:**
44.5 years; **Adult literacy rate:** 33 per
cent; **Access to safe water:** 55 per cent;
**Access to health services:** 80 per cent;
**Access to sanitation:** 21 per cent

## 1 Introduction

The National Environmental Action Plan (NEAP) process in Guinea-Conakry began in 1989 as a result of discussions initiated by the World Bank. The process received considerable financial resources from the Bank, the Canadian International Development Agency (CIDA) and UNDP-UNSO, and 80 staff were quickly recruited to the *Cellule d'appui au plan d'action environmental* (CAPAE). This was located in the Ministry of Natural Resources and Environment, although the dominant sponsor was the now disbanded Ministry of Planning and International Cooperation. Because the rapid expansion of CAPAE was based on monthly retainers many inappropriate 'collaborators' were recruited, most of whom left the NEAP once the retainers were withdrawn. This created an image problem for the NEAP which, combined with the neglect of awareness-raising and institution-building, meant that the first phase of the NEAP process achieved little success.

In retrospect, the NEAP initiative for Guinea-Conakry is considered to have been premature, given the circumstances in the country. The NEAP experienced difficulty in almost every aspect of strategy development and implementation, to the point of rendering the first phase totally ineffective. Lack of political commitment, lack of Guinean technical capacity and exposure to strategy development, an imposed and unrealistic time frame, an excessive focus on project development, restricted participation in the strategy, and inappropriate institutional and management arrangements all combined to mitigate against successful development of the strategy.

Had an assessment of the capacity to undertake strategy development been made to determine the entry point for strategy support, it would have found that significant groundwork was required to raise levels of environmental awareness and achieve the necessary development of human resource capacity. Only then should the full scale strategy development have been undertaken.

## 2 Scope and Objectives

The Guinea-Conakry NEAP process was intended to be national in scope and comprehensive in content. The principles of sustainable development provided the basis for the strategy, with the major objective being the improvement in well-being of the Guinean population.

The strategy set out the following means for achieving this goal:

- human resource development, especially in environmental awareness;
- sustainable development through improved natural resource management; and
- security of biological diversity.

The following principles were meant to guide the strategy process:

- it must be fully participatory at all levels;
- it should be a means to achieve environmental education, training, awareness and policy dialogue;
- all problems and their proposed solutions should be dealt with in an integrated manner;
- it is a long-term initiative with donor support, yet some results must be produced quickly through small experimental actions by the NEAP; and
- it must be built on existing resources such as the Tropical Forestry Action Plan (TFAP) and the Land-Use Plan.

## 3 Relationship to Development Planning

The NEAP process has been poorly integrated into the development planning system and has had virtually no impact on the development planning process. In fact, the work of the NEAP was barely known within government and the majority of the Cabinet did not know of its existence by the end of the first phase.

Despite being attached to the Ministry of Planning and International Cooperation, whose major function was the coordination of investment projects, the NEAP was physically located in the Ministry of Natural Resources and Environment which acted as co-sponsor. This arrangement created resentment on the part of the Environment Ministry which had little control over the NEAP. The resulting conflicts between the two ministries played a major role in the undoing of the first attempt at preparing a strategy for sustainable development in Guinea.

## 4 Initial Development

### Start-Up

Although Guinea-Conakry obtained independence in 1957, it remained under a dictatorship until 1984. Only then did the country begin to address major social and economic problems, which included the collapse of the formal education system, and the loss through emigration of 2.5 million people out of a population of 7 million people.

Up to 1989, Guinea received assistance primarily from UNEP and the UN Food and Agriculture Organization (FAO) to establish an environmental institutional base and develop policy and legislation in a few sectors such as forestry and mining. The TFAP resulted from these efforts in 1989. The concept of a national environment strategy was initiated by the World Bank's African Environment Division (AFTEN) in the spring of 1989. This initiative was accepted and promoted by the then Guinean Minister of Planning, who was a former Bank official, and funds were obtained from the Bank, CIDA and UNDP-UNSO for the initial phase.

*Preparation*

An interministerial unit (CAPAE) was created to take responsibility for the commissioning, implementing, coordinating and administering the NEAP. CAPAE was composed of seven civil servants and was run on a day-to-day basis by a senior civil servant, the Secretary-General of the Ministry of Planning and International Cooperation, who reported to his minister. Other members were middle-level civil servants, representing three different departments. An expatriate technical advisor was provided to assist this unit in the preparation of the NEAP.

None of the seven Guinean members of the CAPAE were seconded full-time to the NEAP. In fact, not even the paid

secretaries were seconded to work full-time on the NEAP. This was attributed to two major factors:

- first, the institutions and persons involved in the NEAP were exclusively governmental. The civil service was therefore the only source of staff. None of the civil servants wished to be seconded full-time to the NEAP because, in the Guinean civil service, post-secondment re-entry to the ministry of origin is not guaranteed.
- second, and perhaps more significantly, the project's resources (material, technical and human) were re-directed by CAPAE's assistant coordinator to a Soviet bauxite project for which he was also responsible. He played a dual role as director of the National Council on the Environment and director of the bauxite project.

The CAPAE recruited 80 civil servants in August–September 1989 to form 11 thematic working groups to prepare papers on the following themes:

- the cost of environmental degradation;
- environmental education;
- land use in areas recently freed from river blindness;
- the institutional and legal framework;
- watershed management;
- the marine and coastal environment;
- the urban environment;

- biodiversity and national parks;
- the mining sector with special focus on plans for iron-ore mining on Mount Njimba;
- environmental information systems and monitoring; and
- environmental impact assessment.

The civil servants involved in these working groups, who received monthly retainers for these services (a crucial consideration given the very low level of government salaries), did not on the whole have appropriate skills. Only a very small percentage had experience in cross-sectoral analysis, and an even smaller percentage had experience in the field of environmental issues. The majority were engineers, particularly mining engineers, as was the assistant coordinator of the CAPAE. There were some social scientists, but no economists. No efforts were made to obtain the missing skills through training or secondments.

By early 1990, donors expressed dissatisfaction with the size of the civil service group, the system of monthly retainers and the poor quality of the few reports that had been produced. They were successful in having the contingent cut by half and the system of monthly retainers replaced by a system of honoraria for specific products. Within a few weeks, only a few stalwarts remained in the

CAPAE, largely on a voluntary and informal basis.

With the help of the technical advisor and a core of regular short-term consultants, the national technicians made a serious attempt to relaunch the NEAP. The main donors backed this renaissance, but the CAPAE management refused to accept the broader and more participatory approach proposed, which would have involved the delegation or sharing of power and financial and physical resources. In the summer of 1991, this small group essentially gave up, thus signalling the end, and the failure of the Phase 1 of the Guinean NEAP.

*Participation in Phase 1*

The approach during Phase One of the NEAP involved little participation or awareness-raising. There was no involve-ment of NGOs or private organizations and CAPAE did not have the legal power to expand its membership beyond the government, nor did it attempt to obtain a change in policy to allow this. NGO involvement was limited to an attempt to create an *ad hoc* NGO for the purpose of representation on the CAPAE and to undertake studies, but this failed. There was no media coverage to speak of, even though the Information Ministry had a representative in the CAPAE.

## 5 Implementation and Results

In early 1990, six months into the NEAP, CAPAE was pressured by the lead donor, the World Bank, to produce a draft strategy document for a Club of Paris donor meeting on Guinea at which the Bank wished to present an action plan focusing on investment projects. It appears that this plan was intended to lead to a major natural resources/environment project which was subsequently developed by the World Bank with FAO in Guinea.

This request for a draft strategy document occurred before the assessment and analysis phase had properly begun. Consequently, despite bringing in a CIDA consultant for a few weeks the resulting strategy document was incomplete with considerable gaps in the areas of population, migration and rural–urban dynamics, rural and urban living conditions, macro- and micro-economics, education and, most importantly, national capacity development. Situations like this pressured production of an initial draft strategy led to one of the most significant weaknesses of the NEAP: its failure to develop technical capacity within government because of externally-imposed time constraints and a focus on quick results which led to the use of external consultants.

Notwithstanding the considerable problems encountered, the Guinean NEAP did produce four well-received studies:

a) a legal and institutional framework study conducted by a consultant from FAO with UNEP financing;
b) a biodiversity action plan developed by IUCN with World Bank financing;
c) a natural resources management plan conducted by a French cooperant in the Forestry Service; and
d) a study on female consumers of natural renewable resources, undertaken by an expatriate consultant with funding from UNSO.

A few other studies were also produced, all by expatriates.

The NEAP process did have some other positive impacts, in particular stimulating a debate around certain key environmental issues in Guinea-Conakry. This came partly from the efforts of the team of technicians, who in the summer of 1990 strained to revive the NEAP, and, in the process, toured three of the four regions of the country. They came back asking fundamental questions, such as:

• Is there real political commitment to the environment, and to the NEAP, in Guinea?
• If so, where are the essential rural poverty alleviation projects that recognize that poverty and resource depletion go hand in hand?

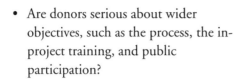

- Are donors serious about wider objectives, such as the process, the in-project training, and public participation?

In addition the team initiated thought and debate on some widespread beliefs about the natural resources situation in Guinea. For example, the team raised the following questions:

- Is erosion in the Fouta Djallon highlands as massive as everyone had been led to believe, to the extent that downstream river systems are affected (Senegal, Gambia and part of the Niger River)? The team expressed serious doubts with respect to this assumption, in light of the fact that erosion in the Fouta Djallon has never been systematically observed or scientifically measured. Vast amounts of funding are provided to that region in the form of projects intended to combat erosion.
- Is Guinea really being 'ravaged' by the mining industry, considering that there are only five industrial mines in a country slightly larger than the United Kingdom?

Thus the NEAP team acted as catalyst for thought and debate on major environmental issues in Guinea-Conakry.

## 6 Lessons Learned

The NEAP process was facilitated by ample financing, with about US$250,000 from the World Bank, the same amount from CIDA, US$100,000 from UNDP-UNEP-UNSO and US$50,000 from other sources – the United States Agency for International Development (USAID) and the United Nations Food and Agriculture Organization (FAO). This permitted the appointment of a resident advisor for two years and the recruitment of short-term international and local consultants. There are few other favourable factors related to the first phase of the Guinean NEAP, however, and many negative influences, which accounted for its poor performance and eventual collapse.

The World Bank was clearly the main proponent of the activity. No one in Guinea had ever heard of an NEAP before it was proposed to the government by the Bank. The major support for the NEAP came from the Bank, CIDA and UNDP, with IUCN acting as a consultant on a specific subject, biodiversity. As a result, the process relied heavily upon external support and never developed the level of domestic support which is necessary for ensuring the long-term momentum and sustainability of the process.

The administrative and institutional set-up for the NEAP proved to have major flaws. CAPAE was at the worst possible level in the hierarchy: too low to exert political influence and too high to actually do anything. Furthermore, control over the project was vested in one person, one of the country's most senior civil servants. The resident technical advisor had no decision-making power. CIDA, who provided financial support for the technical advisor, chose to remain outside of all administrative and financial matters.

The fact that CAPAE was located in the Ministry of Environment, while being responsible to the Ministry of Planning, and that the NEAP process was co-sponsored by these two ministries, rendered the project dependent on the government and good relations between these ministries. The project had little or no autonomy or independence from the country's political pressures.

Another unfavourable factor was that, from its inception, the NEAP suffered from an image problem which, try as it might, it never managed to shed. First, it was run by the Ministry of Planning, whose reputation was already on the wane. Also, the fact that the very first gesture of the CAPAE was to put itself and some 80 officers on monthly retainers on the NEAP budget quickly earned the project a reputation as a *projet-parasite*.

Absence of donor control over the use of project materials, personnel and equipment was a further difficulty. Four different World Bank officers were responsible for the activity over two years; when it became apparent, early in the process, that major management problems needed to be addressed on a day-to-day basis, the Bank attempted in vain to delegate appropriate powers over the NEAP to its Conakry office.

The time frame of 12 to 15 months was inappropriate. For a country with an acute shortage of national technicians and an almost complete lack of vital statistics and baseline studies, it was impossible to produce a comprehensive national environmental strategy in that time. Most importantly, the externally-imposed time frame for the draft NEAP meant that there was no time to train staff and develop the necessary technical capacity within government to sustain the NEAP process as should occur in a strategy development process. Further, the emphasis of the NEAP process on the quick production of a portfolio of projects meant that the strategic nature of the process was compromised, with excessive attention paid to project formulation and insufficient attention to the development of the strategic planning capacity within government.

Technical assistance for the NEAP was uneven. Except for the originator of the project in the World Bank, no one associated with the project had any relevant operational experience of the preparation of an NEAP or an NCS. Thus the NEAP group in Conakry was largely left to fend for itself; for example, a full year went by before they saw an environmental action plan or a national conservation strategy document.

The most important lesson from the Guinea-Conakry NEAP experience is that a careful assessment of the capacity within a country to undertake the development of a strategy must be made before the strategy process is launched. It must be recognized that not all countries are ready to go straight into the development and implementation of a strategy.

The results of such an assessment in Guinea-Conakry would have determined the appropriate point of entry with respect to the preparation of the strategy. Had this been done, it would have been apparent that resources were sorely lacking and that an important capacity-building phase should have been energetically pursued before the main strategy work was initiated. Guinea-Conakry had neither the political commitment nor the human resource capability to enter directly into the process of strategy development and implementation.

The preliminary phase also should have included the discussion of environmental issues with the goal of raising levels of environmental consciousness among key decision makers. Key technical individuals could have been trained to strengthen the necessary analytical skills needed for strategy development. Indicators to monitor progress in capacity development could also have been developed and agreed upon by the parties.

An assessment of the level of political support for an NEAP is also critical. If support is found to be lacking at the highest level, it is certain to be difficult to obtain sufficient political support in the lower echelons of government. In the case of Guinea, lack of solid political support had the following consequences:

- the impact of debate and questioning of key issues on the part of the NEAP team never got beyond a small group of specialists, mostly expatriates, working in the capital city;
- the institutional location and administrative procedures were inadequate, with the NEAP not attached to the right institution, totally dependent on government, and having insufficient administrative control;
- donor efforts to redress the situation proved inadequate because of the lack of high-level political support; and

- efforts by the project team to obtain support from the NGO community, the private sector and religious officials were also hindered by the lack of political support.

As a result of the various problems which the NEAP encountered the overall impact of the first phase has been both disappointing and counter-productive, with many problems and heritages created which now have to be addressed before progress towards sustainability can be institutionalized.

## 7  Chronology

| | |
|---|---|
| 1957 | Independence for Guinea-Conakry. |
| 1957–84 | Dictatorship government of Sekou Toure. |
| 1983 | Earthquake in Gaoual prefecture. |
| 1985 | Economic Reform and Recovery Plan, and Structural Adjustment Plan developed, ongoing to date. |
| 1986 | Department of Natural Resources and Environment established; National Environment Agency established. |
| 1987 | National Environmental Council established; adoption of the Environmental Code. |
| 1987–88 | Elaboration of Tropical Forestry Action Plan. |
| 1988 | World Bank approaches Minister of Planning to undertake an NEAP. Toxic waste dumped on island off Conakry; international uproar. |
| 1989 | World Bank supports the initial phases of an NEAP. |
| | CAPAE set up to undertake NEAP in the Ministry of Environment and Natural Resources. |
| | August–September: 80 civil servants are recruited, put on retainers to work in 11 working groups. Background papers are undertaken. |
| 1990 | Donors express objection to size of the civil service contingent in CAPAE, and have the group cut by half. Major refugee flow into Guinea from civil war in neighbouring Liberia; considerable environmental impact. |
| 1991 | Remaining technical group in CAPAE gives up work on the NEAP. |
| 1992 | The Ministry of Planning is abolished. Revival of NEAP by a new mixed government–donor–NGO grouping; an NGO, *Guinée-Ecologie*, is the chief executing agency. |

# *Kenya*

## *EAP-ASAL and NEAP*

VERITY M NYAGAH, MINISTRY OF
ENVIRONMENT AND NATURAL
RESOURCES; AND GEORGE O KHRODA,
ENVIRONMENTAL ADVISOR EAP-ASAL

**Estimated population 1992:** 25.4
million; **Land area:** 570,000 km²;
**Ecological zones:** Lake Victoria basin,
Central Rift highlands, eastern plateau,
coastal belt, northern arid and semi-arid
region; **Climate:** semi-desert in the north,
tropical on the coast; **Annual rainfall:**
250–1200 mm; **Forest and woodland
area:** 22,800 km²; **GNP per capita:**
US$330; **Main industries:** agriculture,
food processing, textiles, chemicals; **ODA
received per capita:** US$35.20;
**Population growth rate** (1992–2000):
3.1 per cent; **Life expectancy at birth:**
55.7 years; **Adult literacy rate:** 74.5 per
cent; **Access to safe water:** 49 per cent;
**Access to health services:** 77 per cent;
**Access to sanitation:** 43 per cent

*Background*

Concern for environmental planning has a long history in Kenya. The need to integrate environment and economic development was recognized in the country's development plans as far back as 1974. The 1974–78 plan noted increased competition and conflict between land-use interests, and recommended greater coordination between the various arms of government in order to address these problems effectively. The subsequent plan for the 1979–1983 period stressed the need for environmental inputs to be a requirement of the planning machinery in the country and pointed out that 'environmental considerations must come to pervade development decisions at every level'.

While Kenya has seen a large number of initiatives in the natural resources sector, with master plans for river basins and particular resources, there was no strategic or integrated approach related to the environment until 1989 when the preparation of an Environmental Action Plan for the Arid and Semi-Arid Lands was commenced. This was followed in 1993 by the launching of the NEAP. The importance of this is reflected in the 1994–96 Development Plan, which calls for a government sessional paper on sustainable development in order to set comprehensive guidelines and strategies for government action, building on the NEAP process.

# Environmental Action Plan for Arid and Semi-Arid Lands

## 1 Introduction

Arid and semi-arid lands (ASAL) in Kenya cover some 88 per cent of the country's land area and support more than 25 per cent of its population and half of its livestock. They also include more than 95 per cent of the area of national parks and game reserves. Of the 46 districts in Kenya, 24 are categorized as ASAL districts. Many of Kenya's most intractable environment and development problems are found there.

Kenya's strategy for ASAL includes the formulation, adoption and implementation of:

- a Development Policy for the Arid and Semi-Arid Lands;
- an Environmental Action Plan for Arid and Semi-Arid Lands (EAP-ASAL);
- a Human Resources Development and Institutional Capacity-Building Plan; and
- an ASAL Development Programme.

The Development Policy for ASAL and the EAP-ASAL document were completed and adopted by the Ministry of Reclamation and Development of Arid, Semi-Arid Areas and Wastelands (MRDASW) in 1992. The EAP-ASAL has subsequently become a building block in the NEAP. Besides the overall EAP-ASAL, there are District-Specific Environmental Action Plans (DS-EAPs) for the 24 ASAL districts. These districts have diverse characteristics, and differ widely in their natural resource endowment, level of use, extent of environmental degradation, and stage of development. Each DS-EAP document provides a detailed assessment of the district's natural resources, development trends, opportunities and constraints.

The EAP-ASAL, which includes pro-grammes of action and priorities for the ASAL districts, was formulated in 1992. It was discussed by the District Develop-ment Committees in line with the Government of Kenya (GOK)'s District Focus for Rural Development. The intention was that the EAP-ASAL should be implemented through the DS-EAPs. In 1992, however, the MRDASW was merged with the Ministry of Water Development and the Ministry of Regional Development into what is presently known as the Ministry of Land Reclamation, Regional and Water Development (MLRRWD). The portfolio of MRDASW is presently represented by the Department of Land Reclamation in the expanded ministry.

Implementation of the various initiatives for the ASAL has been hampered by the merger of the ministries. In addition, unresolved issues, such as a lack of interagency coordination, a narrowly sectoral approach, an absence of capacity-building in the Ministry of Land Reclamation, as well as inadequate participation by NGOs and local communities, have also delayed implementation. Nonetheless, the ideas generated by the EAP-ASAL and the DS-EAPs have been incorporated into the National Development Plan, the NEAP and the District Development Plans of the 24 ASAL districts.

## 2 Scope and Objectives

The EAP-ASAL provides a sub-national framework for district-specific environmental action plans in 24 of Kenya's 46 districts. The overall objective is to enhance the ability of the ASAL communities to manage their resources in a sustainable manner. Specific objectives included in the EAP are:

- encouraging ASAL communities in the sound management of rangelands for better livestock production;
- assisting ASAL communities in developing a sustainable agro-pastoral economy;
- assisting the integration of wildlife and tourism into the economies of ASAL inhabitants;

- increasing the supply of water to ASAL areas using methods that are environmentally and economically sustainable;
- promoting the sustainable exploitation of wood resources;
- improving the physical infrastructure in ASAL to boost overall access, particularly access to markets and services;
- increasing the ASAL communities' awareness of environmental issues;
- preparing for future drought and possible famine;
- reclaiming wastelands and restoring their ecological productivity; and
- promoting environmentally-friendly indigenous technologies and training for ASAL communities.

The strategy is guided by three basic principles:

- all people living in the ASAL should be assisted in obtaining their right to an environment adequate for their health and well-being;
- the environment and its natural resources should be used sustainably for the benefit of both present and future generations, so as to preserve biodiversity and maintain essential ecosystems;
- local knowledge and technologies should be valued and utilized to ensure that the development of the ASAL benefits, and responds to the needs of, the local population.

*55*

## 3 Relationship to Development Planning

MRDASW was responsible for both development planning and environmental management of the ASAL. Theoretically speaking, the EAP-ASAL strategy was well integrated with the development planning system in that ministry. MRDASW mandate was not well integrated with the rest of the government ministries and departments, however, and there were significant gaps and duplication of effort.

MRDASW was set up in 1989 to coordinate ASAL projects because the flow of funds for these projects was beginning to overwhelm existing ministries. Although there was a large amount of money in the ministry for projects, little was budgeted for running MRDASW or for building its capacity for strategic planning and project management.

Although the EAP-ASAL provides a strategic, intersectoral basis for planning and coordination, it only provides this framework for one ecological region of the country. Hence, this initiative failed to break away from the tendency in Kenya to develop master plans which focus on particular sectors, such as forestry and water, or in this case arid lands, and so reinforced the lack of an adequate nationwide framework of strategic and intersectoral planning and coordination. In addition, like many of the master plans,

the EAP-ASAL was developed to a considerable degree at the behest of the donors, and was not well rooted in MRDASW.

## 4 Strategy Development

Concern for the ASAL dates back to 1979 when the GOK realized that the ASAL included the major frontiers of development in the country, and that their environments were becoming more fragile. This concern led to the preparation of a policy document entitled 'The Arid and Semi-Arid Lands of Kenya: A Framework for Implementation, Programme Planning and Evaluation'. This was meant to guide project planning, implementation and management of development activities in ASAL. Subsequently, the number of ASAL projects increased, but the standard of living of the local people did not improve much, and environmental degradation continued.

While the framework for implementation drew some attention to the ASAL it failed to provide a coherent and strategic policy governing the planning, implementation and management of projects in the ASAL. Consequently, in 1989 the GOK established MRDASW with the mandate to protect ASAL ecosystems and develop opportunities for achieving a sustainable quality of life, creating employment and attaining food security. To fulfil this

mandate, MRDASW began formulating a development policy for ASAL, an EAP for ASAL and DS-EAPs.

The preparation of the EAP-ASAL was commissioned by MRDASW. The work was initially contracted to externally-recruited consultants but there were a number of problems with the first two drafts. Hence, in 1991, MRDASW requested the World Bank ASAL team to finalize the EAP-ASAL document and formulate the district-specific EAPs for the 24 ASAL districts. This team consisted of an economist, a rural sociologist, and a natural resource management specialist, provided and funded by the governments of Germany, the Netherlands and Kenya, UNSO and the World Bank.

The ASAL team prepared a third draft of the EAP, which was discussed at a two-day workshop in 1991. The workshop was attended by representatives of government departments, donor agencies and some NGOs. After the workshop, comments and amendments were received by the ASAL team and incorporated in the fourth draft. This was reviewed by a small number of GOK representatives and donor agencies, while a fifth draft was discussed with senior officials of MRDASW, and adopted by it with minor changes in 1992.

The EAP-ASAL document describes the ASAL and diagnoses their key environ-mental issues with respect to demographic trends, land-use trends and conflicts, and degradation of natural resources. It considers the current policy and institutional framework, including the implementing and coordinating organiza-tions, and the existing environmental legislation. It sets out an EAP, including policies, organizations, capacity-building, community participation, sectoral actions, and multi-sectoral activities.

The ASAL Team also prepared the Development Policy for ASAL and formu-lated a Human Resources Development and Institutional Capacity Building Project, Guidelines for Land Use and Land Tenure in ASAL and an overall ASAL Development Programme. The latter was intended to be an overall investment plan for the ASAL DS-EAPs and included the programmes of action for each district. The plans intended to use the regular district machinery for planning, implementation and management of projects, ie the District Development Committees. These consist of the District Commissioner (chair), the District Environmental Officer, district officials from the line ministries (extension and/or technical officials), representatives of district-based NGOs, and represen-tatives of donor agencies operating in the district.

Participation in the formulation of the DS-EAPs was largely limited to national and district government officials and donor agencies. Although NGOs are members of District Development Committees, few of them attend. The main reason for the lack of NGO involvement is that there is no tradition of cooperation between the government and NGOs.

## 5 Implementation and Results

Progress with the implementation of the EAP-ASAL has been mixed. One of the causes of failure in the implementation process has been the continuous change of institutional arrangements. First, the key implementing ministry, MRDASW, was merged with two other ministries, those of water development and regional development. The MRDASW became a department after the merger and, within the larger ministry, emphasis shifted from ASAL development to water development. In this regard, ASAL programmes have suffered a lack of attention.

With the ministry no longer in place, the ASAL investment programme was reduced and diverted to constitute the present World Bank-funded Arid Lands Project. Some elements of the ASAL investment programme were incorporated in the World Bank-funded Drought Emergency Project, and the Drought Monitoring and Management Programme funded by the Netherlands government, but many aspects have been neglected. Integrating

the EAP-ASAL with other ongoing programmes has not been very successful, as ideas and projects from the EAP for ASAL have been picked up in an *ad hoc* manner by donor projects and government programmes. Hence the strategic perspective has been lost.

One area of success has been in the formulation of the National Development Plan for 1994–1996. In this current plan, issues raised in the EAP-ASAL have been addressed and solutions suggested. Because of this action at the national level, there has been support from the district administrations in following up the ideas from the EAP-ASAL.

In addition, because the DS-EAPs were locally formulated, their basic ideas appear to have been included in the District Development Plans. This process has been assisted by posting District Environment Officers from the President's Office, with political clout as a strong support for their activities. As a result there have been attempts to implement, or at least share, the ideas that were formula-ted in these plans, and greater awareness has been created at local levels.

The current sectoral plans, such as the Water Master Plan and Forestry Master Plan, have also incorporated some of the fundamental issues raised in the EAP-ASAL. However, implementation is still awaited in many of these sectors.

The formulation of the NEAP also appears to have taken into account most of the actions proposed in the EAP-ASAL. (The development and implementation of the NEAP is discussed later in this chapter.)

In addition, the following programmes will apply the ideas from the EAP-ASAL in greater depth in specific areas:

• the Desertification Action Plan;
• the Biological Diversity Action Plan; and
• the Climate Change Action Plan.

These are now on the drawing board as follow-ups to the EAP-ASAL or as a result of the NEAP initiative. They will address these issues in much greater detail than was possible in either the EAP-ASAL or the NEAP.

## 6 Lessons Learned

Despite the failure to implement the EAP-ASAL in total there has been some progress made and some lessons learned.

### Strengths

With the formulation of the DS-EAPs it was possible to include some of the proposed actions in the District Development Plans. The District Environment Officers, therefore, have some guidance concerning the issues requiring their attention. Development agents appear to have found several ideas useful, although this cannot be confirmed because there is little acknowledgement of the EAP-ASAL as the source of their ideas. The NEAP has taken up most of the issues raised in the EAP-ASAL and taken them further within a national framework.

### Weaknesses

Weak and unclear institutional arrangements have delayed implementation. In particular, the merger of MRDASW with two other ministries led to a lack of support and has greatly weakened implementation of programmes and projects in the EAP-ASAL.

The narrowness of the EAP-ASAL approach, in terms of its focus upon one ecological zone, has made it liable to criticism and has reduced long-term support for it. There has been a decline in donor support as UNSO, which funded the resource management sector, has scaled down its operations since 1994. Also, a shift of focus to the NEAP has occurred, in part because it appears to be well funded, and has an able secretariat and strong political support.

*Lessons*

The political climate did not support free and frank discussions over the EAP-ASAL. As a result, participation was limited to representatives of the GOK and donor agencies.

Sub-regional plans appear to be thwarted by a lack of national support. Evidence suggests that institutional, legislative and administrative instruments that are necessary for implementation need to be enacted at national levels.

There has been poor coordination by the GOK during the formulation process and by donor agencies during the implementation process. Donors, in particular, carry out more activities than government and have created parallel projects.

The battle between breadth and detail in designing the EAP-ASAL resulted in compromises which have led to inaction. In addition, the presence of strong sectoral planning in Kenya has hindered a regional or ecological zone approach.

## 7 Issues

The experience with the EAP-ASAL raises a number of issues relevant to strategy development. Seven are reviewed below.

*Scope*

The strategy's sub-national scope has made it very difficult to promote changes that are applicable nationwide. For example, the ASAL strategy has been limited to proposing guidelines on land use instead of developing a comprehensive land-use policy, because national policy on land use is the responsibility of the Ministry of Lands and Settlements. In practice, land-use policy consists of sectoral laws on how particular lands may be used (for example, the Agriculture Act, Wildlife Protection Act, etc). A comprehensive land-use policy is needed, especially now that competing resource uses are beginning to create much conflict.

*Formulation*

Although the EAP for ASAL is a good starting point and provides a useful assessment of environmental issues, it still has to contend with some serious weaknesses. The process of formulating the EAP revealed a lack of intersectoral consultation and coordination. The Ministry of Lands and Settlement was working on a 'Sessional Paper on Agricultural Land-Use Policy', while the Kenya Wildlife Service was organizing a land-use study. Overlapping master plans on water and forestry have also been prepared. There was no communication element within the EAP-

ASAL formulation process. As a result there was no attempt to exchange views, coordinate programmes, or harmonize actions. No serious effort was made to offer guidelines for resolving interagency conflicts, although they are a major cause of unsustainable use and mismanagement of resources.

*Analysis*

The EAP-ASAL document does not critically assess the GOK's commitment to the strategy. Its analysis of the policy and institutional framework is weak. The legal framework for environmental management is inadequate and the necessary legislation has been stalled. The National Environment Secretariat in the Ministry of Environment and Natural Resources and MRDASW were poorly staffed and under-funded. MRDASW, in particular, depended on donor funds for most of its operations. Ongoing actions were not assessed for the strategy; although such an assessment is a necessary step to the planning of required actions, and is also an informative and appropriate way of evaluating government commitment.

*Participation*

The lack of participation by NGOs and local communities has hindered the implementation process. One major strength of the strategy is its district focus,

but this has been provided almost entirely by officials alone. If the GOK wishes to facilitate development, many tasks at the local level will have to be implemented by the communities themselves or by local NGOs. The debate about the NGOs Registration Act has created more suspicion instead of drawing NGOs toward the government as partners in the development process.

*Lack of Context*

The EAP-ASAL document does not discuss the lessons learned from previous efforts to develop sustainably in the ASAL. In the past two decades, there have been several integrated ASAL projects which could offer insights on technologies and experiences that are both economically sustainable and ecologically friendly. As such, the strategy does not take advantage of proven technologies and methods for ASAL development.

In contrast, the team which developed the NEAP has paid more attention to learning lessons from previous experience and developed a more consultative and participatory mechanism for the development of that strategic plan.

Inadequate environmental legislation and land-use policy are the key constraints to the implementation of EAP-ASAL. The GOK plans to set up a land-use commission during the National Development Plan period (1994/6) and the environmental legislation produced as a result of joint EAP-ASAL and NEAP activities is already in draft form and under discussion.

### *Capacity Development*

Training and skill development had been envisaged during the formulation of the EAP-ASAL. However, the operationalisation of capacity development was delayed because the plan dealt with the issues of human resources development at a broad level and failed to make specific recommendations. In addition, overall capacity building was seen to be implemented through programmes that were to be funded as projects emanating from the plan itself (because the plan as a whole has been a non-starter, the entire capacity-building aspect has suffered).

### *Monitoring and Assessment*

No monitoring and evaluation programme was established for the EAP-ASAL. This was partly because the Danish International Development Agency

(DANIDA) had posted an expert in MRDASW who had the mandate to establish a monitoring procedure for all the projects in the Ministry, including the EAP-ASAL. However, this task was not completed before the Ministry was dissolved.

## 8 *Conclusions*

While the EAP-ASAL has not been implemented in its own right, there is no doubt that formulation of this strategy has contributed considerably to the development of strategic environmental management in Kenya. Ideas from this plan have filtered into the District Development Plans and into the activities of the District Environmental Officers and some of the line ministries in the ASAL. In addition, the EAP-ASAL put on the agenda a number of issues which the NEAP was able to pick up and raise at the national level. Finally, it should be noted that the EAP-ASAL has contributed to an attitudinal change, first with the development implementers in the districts and also with the decision makers, helping to place environmental issues on the agenda for consideration.

# National Environmental Action Plan

## 1 Origins

Kenya's National Environmental Action Plan (NEAP) process was launched on 29 and 30 June 1993 at a workshop organized by the Ministry of Environment and Natural Resources (MENR). The NEAP was developed at this time in response to a number of influences. Most notable was the wish of the GOK, after the 1992 United Nations Conference on Environment and Development (UNCED), to reactivate strategic environmental planning. Planning had been initiated in 1991 with IUCN but the government had not reached any conclusion about how to proceed. MENR was also encouraged to take up the NEAP process because of an offer from the World Bank, initially through the Ministry of Finance, to provide a project preparation facility grant for the development of a strategic environmental plan. The donor required an NEAP to be in place if the country was to be eligible for the grant.

## 2 The NEAP Process

The 1993 workshop, which initiated the NEAP process in Kenya, was attended by more than 100 representatives from government ministries and departments, the private sector, NGOs, and bilateral and multilateral agencies. Participants at the two-day meeting were formed into five working groups and were asked to make recommendations about areas of concern. The recommendations, which originally numbered 22, were later consolidated into nine thematic areas, forming the core of the NEAP activity. These were:

- policy, institutional and legislative framework, including economic incentives;
- biodiversity, including forestry and wildlife;
- water resources, including inland water resources, coastal and marine resources;
- environmental pollution control and waste management;
- human settlements and urbanization;
- community participation and public awareness;
- desertification and drought;
- sustainable agriculture and food security; and
- a national environmental information system.

Following the initial workshop, an NEAP Secretariat was established in September 1993. The Secretariat is headed by a Coordinator, who is assisted by a Deputy Coordinator and a team of 11 support staff. The Secretariat is located in the Ministry of the Environment and all staff are drawn from that Ministry. The Secretariat is at a relatively high level within the Ministry and reports directly to the Permanent Secretary.

The operational activities of the NEAP process commenced on 1 November 1993 with the establishment of nine task forces, whose responsibility was to prepare issues papers for the nine thematic areas mentioned above. The preparation of the issues papers was an open and interactive process with the task forces and their sub-groups, working with a wide range of people including academicians and representatives of NGOs, the private sector and the public sector. To a large extent the work of the task forces was one of consolidating and harmonizing existing information found in documents such as the Forestry Master Plan, the Water Master Plan, and the Strategy for the Arid and Semi-Arid Lands. Each task force met on a regular, often weekly, basis over the period November 1993 to April 1994 for discussions of the work which its sub-groups were undertaking. While much of the work was based on analysis of existing documentation, most task forces undertook discussions with senior

managers with particular environmental responsibilities. Some task forces were also involved with field visits to obtain the current views of key groups in Kenyan society concerning particular issues, such as incentives for clean technology in industry.

To ensure the objective of broad participation and consultation in the process, regional workshops were organized in each of the country's five provinces. These involved a total of over 300 participants from different government departments in each district (such as development, environment, water, forestry and agriculture) and from particular communities and interest groups (such as farmers', women's and catchment conservation groups). On the first day of each workshop an initial draft of the issues in each thematic area was presented by two people from each task force. These were then discussed by the participants in four working groups, which focused on:

- natural resources and agriculture;
- policy issues;
- community participation and awareness; and
- human settlements.

The workshops generated a very open and informative debate which not only helped raise public understanding of the NEAP process but also elicited many comments and recommendations which strengthened the issues papers. The task force reports were revised in the light of these workshops and then discussed and reviewed by an interministerial and intersectoral technical committee in May 1994 under the chairmanship of the Minister for Environment and Natural Resources. These final reports provided the basis for two professional editors to compile the NEAP under the guidance of the NEAP Coordinating Committee.

## 3 Recommendations of the NEAP

The NEAP was officially approved by the GOK on 29 July 1994. The NEAP document lays out a number of important principles underlying an effective environmental policy and strategy. These include:

- harmonization of legislation;
- use of economic incentives and disincentives to encourage positive environmental action;
- use of across-the-board environmental assessments procedure;
- formulation of a comprehensive policy for land use and settlements;
- greater community involvement in environmental and natural resource management; and
- emphasis on environmental education and the need for international cooperation.

As an essential prerequisite, the NEAP calls for a strengthening of the institutional framework, including the need for an independent agency, backed by supporting legislation, to ensure coordination of environmental policy and management. Finally, it defines some priority areas for sectoral and cross-sectoral action, such as the need to develop a national environmental information system, and a biodiversity strategy.

While the NEAP did make recommendations concerning the form of institutional development necessary to coordinate environmental matters and integrate them into national economic development planning, the precise nature and location of the institutional development recommendation could not be agreed by the NEAP Workshop and Executive Committee. As a result this remains a matter for consideration in the current Phase 2 of the NEAP process which is secure of funding to the end of 1997.

## 4 Implementation of the NEAP: Recommendations

The Minister of Finance incorporated some of the NEAP recommendations in his budget speech on 16 June 1994 and the subsequent Finance Bill which he tabled in Parliament. This Finance Bill provides for tax reductions for machinery and equipment that will be utilized for environmental clean-up operations, including disposal of effluent and other wastes. While this was a sign of government commitment to implement the NEAP, there has been variable progress on the four major prerequisites for implementation.

### *Sessional Policy Paper on Sustainable Development*

The policy paper on sustainable development, recommended by the 1994–96 National Plan and supported by the NEAP, has been finalized and is pending approval from the government. It has been developed by a Select Committee of 20 members drawn from the public sector, the NGO community, and the private sector. The members of this Committee have been selected by the Office of the President and the Committee has worked within the MENR. Once approved by Cabinet, this paper will go to Parliament for approval and will become government policy. It seems likely that this paper will support the role of the NEAP in integrating environmental considerations into the National Development Planning Process.

### *Development of the Environment Management and Coordination Bill*

The Attorney General established an Experts Committee to develop an Environmental Management and Coordination Bill based on the recommendations of NEAP. The Committee finalized the first draft in August 1995 and a workshop was held in early September to discuss the draft.

This draft is subject to revision in the light of the findings of a study commissioned by the NEAP Secretariat which is reviewing the institutional options for environmental management in Kenya as a follow-up to the NEAP recommendations. The study will incorporate personnel requirements and costs associated with each of the options. Detailed analysis will also be carried out on the linkages of the different options with the District Development Committees, especially the line ministries in the field, NGOs, local communities, etc.

### *Environmental Impact Assessment Programme*

The development of EIA guidelines and procedures was initiated in September

1994 following the establishment of an interministerial/intersectoral committee. To address specific sectoral guidelines, the committee has been divided into five sub-committees: agriculture, transportation, natural resources and tourism, industry, infrastructure and human settlements. A number of field exercises were organized for the sub-committees. These field trips have focused on current development projects. Experience from the field will be incorporated in the draft guidelines.

### Environmental Management Project

In addition to the above components, the NEAP Secretariat is in the process of discussing the development of an Environment Management Project with the World Bank. This will consist of a series of sub-projects based on analysis of the ongoing situation in the NEAP document.

## 5  Lessons Learned

The NEAP process in Kenya has a number of clear strengths.

### Participation

The principle of broad participation of stakeholders was followed right from the start, although this was based on selection of participants at the workshops by government officials. This participatory approach provides a framework for continuous dialogue thus facilitating inter-sectoral collaboration. It also increases the awareness of the different stakeholders, thus making it possible to have effective and more integrated decision making.

### Holistic Analysis

The NEAP process has stressed the cross-sectoral nature of the causes of environmental degradation, including the impact of policy and institutional constraints.

### Analysis of Existing Information

The NEAP process has used available information and skilled staff. This recognizes the need to build upon existing experience and to strengthen national capacity.

### Harmonization

Attention has been given to the harmonization of the existing plans and policies in the environmental sub-sectors within the NEAP. In this way the NEAP process may provide an initial forum for the coordination of environmental projects.

### Environmental Monitoring

There has been a recognition, as a result of the NEAP process, of the need to undertake systematic efforts to understand the state of the environment and to monitor its change.

### Coordination with Donors

The establishment of an NEAP Advisory Committee, with donor representation, has provided a forum by means of which the donors have been kept appraised of the NEAP developments. This has been important in the identification of financial support for specific activities and projects recommended by the NEAP.

### Training

Under the NEAP Training component, participants from the public and private sectors, NGOs and research institutions have been beneficiaries of training programmes in Integrated Environmental Management and Tools for Environmental Assessment.

At the same time the NEAP has encountered a number of weaknesses which require further attention.

### Economic Analysis

The limited economic analysis and use of natural resource valuation within the NEAP has left this process with a major area of weakness.

### Integrating the NEAP into Economic Planning

Despite the NEAP originating as a result of an initiative from the Ministry of Finance, which is closely linked with the Ministry of Planning and National Development, there has been little progress in integrating the NEAP recommendations into the country's macro-economic framework. As a result the NEAP has remained a parallel planning process. This should not be the case and the NEAP should be fully integrated into the overall macro-economic framework.

### People's Perspectives

There is a need to improve the link between environmental conservation and the aspirations of the people for better opportunities and living conditions.

### Implementation and Integration

The progress from development to implementation of the NEAP has been slow. The policy paper is still awaiting Cabinet approval and the institutional arrangements are still being assessed. This situation shows the limited power of the MENR, as a sectoral ministry, to push the NEAP process forward, especially in the areas of integrating the recommendations into the overall macro-economic framework.

## 6 General Conclusions

The experience of the EAP-ASAL and the NEAP show a progression in environmental planning in Kenya. While both have been important in introducing an holistic approach to environmental issues, rather than following the traditional sectoral approach, the NEAP was especially important in moving to a national perspective. Hence the NEAP marks a turning point.

However, getting the holistic approach to environmental issues onto the agenda is not sufficient. This needs to be operationalized and integrated into the country's planning and development system if it is to have any significant impact upon the long-term sustainability of Kenyan communities and their economies. Such operationalisation of the EAP-ASAL was achieved in some degree through the DS-EAPs and through the activities of the District Environment Officers. The challenge for the NEAP is to ensure that all line ministries pick up the principles which it has outlined and apply these in their work and encourage the private sector to follow them. While the NEAP marks a major step forward in Kenyan environmental activities, it is, as yet, only a starting point on which much must be built.

## 7  Chronology

| | |
|---|---|
| 1989 | GOK establishes the Ministry of Reclamation and Development of Arid, Semi-Arid Areas and Wastelands (MRDASW). |
| 1990 | April: First draft of the EAP-ASAL document prepared. |
| | July: Second draft of the EAP-ASAL document prepared. |
| 1991 | May: MRDASW and World Bank agree on terms of reference for the World Bank ASAL Team to complete the EAP-ASAL document and formulate district-specific EAPs for the then 21 ASAL districts (since then, three more districts have been established). |
| 1992 | July: Workshop discusses third draft of the EAP-ASAL document. |
| | August: Fourth draft of the EAP-ASAL document prepared. |
| | October: Development Policy for ASAL adopted by MRDASW. Fifth draft of the EAP-ASAL document discussed with senior officials of MRDASW. |
| | November: EAP-ASAL document adopted by MRDASW with minor changes. |
| | MRDASW merged with Ministries of Water Development and Regional Development. |
| 1993 | June: NEAP process initiated. |
| 1993–94 | Incorporation of some of EAP-ASAL ideas into 1994–96 National Development Plan. |
| 1994 | July: NEAP presented to the government. |
| | September: EIA Programme initiated. |
| 1995 | Sessional paper on sustainable development prepared. |
| | August: Environmental Management and Coordination Bill drafted. |

# Lesotho

*National Environmental Action Plan*

AAH SEKHESA, NATIONAL ENVIRONMENT
SECRETARIAT

**Estimated population 1992:** 1.9 million;
**Land area:** 30,355 km²; **Ecological
zones:** mountains (Drakensberg Range,
Maloti spurs), plateau (source of Tugela
and Orange rivers), lowlands; **Climate:**
mild and dry winters; warm summer
season (October–April); **Annual rainfall:**
725 mm; **GNP per capita:** US$610;
**Main industries:** agriculture, wool,
tourism; **ODA received per capita:**
US$67.90; **Population growth rate
(1992–2000):** 2.7 per cent; **Life
expectancy at birth:** 60.5 years; **Adult
literacy rate:** 68.6 per cent; **Access to safe
water:** 47 per cent; **Access to health
services:** 80 per cent; **Access to
sanitation:** 22 per cent

## 1 Introduction

Lesotho is a small land-locked country surrounded by South Africa. It has a land area of 30,355 square kilometres. Of this, only nine per cent is estimated to be arable land suitable for agriculture, while some 60 per cent is suitable for grazing and the remaining 31 per cent for settlement development. Due to the topography, the country has four distinct ecological regions, ranging from 1400m to 3400m above sea level.

The country's population is estimated at 1.9 million people, with an annual growth rate of 2.7 per cent. The country has a limited natural resource base with the exception of water, which it has in abundance. The population growth rate, although not high when compared to other countries in Africa, presents serious environmental and developmental challenges because it is not in balance with the natural resource base. Furthermore, the inability of the economy to absorb the growing labour force and the heavy economic dependence on South Africa makes the country vulnerable to circumstances beyond its control.

As the population increases annually, more people in Lesotho are becoming dependent on land for their livelihood. There is a resultant deterioration in the quality of the scarce land resources due to over-exploitation. In fact, it is acknowledged in various publications that the link between environment and development in Lesotho is all too clear and the question of sustainability should be a concern for both present and future generations because impoverishment of the country's land base has taken on the dimension of a crisis.

The most critical environmental problems have been identified as:

• land degradation due to overstocking and deterioration of rangelands;
• soil erosion and fertility loss contributing to scarred gullies and dongas;
• rapid urbanization rate and unplanned settlement development encroaching into the scarce arable land and contributing to declining agricultural production;
• water pollution due to hazardous use of agricultural chemicals and indiscriminate disposal of both liquid and solid waste; and
• loss of natural and historical heritage.

## 2 Development Phase

Lesotho was one of the first countries in sub-Saharan Africa to prepare an NEAP. This was begun in 1988 with the assistance of the World Bank, and was adopted by the government in 1989. The NEAP marked an important initiative for Lesotho as it provided a framework for the integration of environmental considerations into the planning and decision-making processes for social and economic development, and further increased awareness of environmental issues in the country.

The NEAP was prepared through a long process which involved consultations from the village to the national level. Consultations were held with Village Development Councils, traditional leaders (chiefs), District Development Councils and all major stakeholders in the country. A major conference was held in April 1988 to discuss the issues that had emanated from the district consultations, and from the supporting documents and literature that already existed. The conference participants included senior government officials, NGOs, District Development Councils, chiefs, and all other major actors. The resulting plan identified the areas of environmental concern which are of highest priority to Lesotho and specified the actions necessary to address these areas. It further defined principles for the National Environmental Policy for Lesotho, as well as the institutional and legislative structures to implement the policy.

A preliminary draft of the plan was prepared and translated into Sesotho for circulation and comments. Thereafter external experts together with local experts revised the document for final presentation to the government.

Although the NEAP was a very important initiative in addressing environmental issues in Lesotho, there was no follow-up attempt to implement its recommendations until 1994 when, with the assistance of the United Nations Development Programme (UNDP), the Government of Lesotho revisited the plan, and a proposal for implementation was made. A one-week workshop was held in May 1995 to review the NEAP; this culminated in the preparation of a more comprehensive action plan for the implementation of Agenda 21 in Lesotho. The Agenda 21 National Action Plan builds on the foundations of the NEAP and aims to achieve close inter-agency coordination and cooperation for the implementation of national plans on environment and natural resources management.

The preparation of the Agenda 21 National Action Plan has been similarly broad-based, with the involvement of different actors including senior government officers, members of Parliament and Senate, NGOs, private sector, women's groups, professional associations, youth groups, etc. After the one-week workshop of intensive discussions, the National Environment Secretariat (established in April 1994), together with an international consultant, prepared the draft report. This was widely circulated for comments, and thereafter a final report was prepared and presented to the government for adoption. The plan has now been translated into Sesotho, and meetings have been held with the district authorities to sensitize them and get their views on its contents. The long-term objective is that district authorities will ultimately prepare their own District Environmental Action Plans, whereby they will articulate their problems, list possible remedial actions and indicate their commitment to the implementation of these plans.

In order to achieve improved environment and natural resources management, the National Environment Secretariat is also giving priority to education and promoting public awareness to the different groups in society. In this regard an outreach programme on environmental education has been embarked upon through newspapers in both English and Sesotho, radio and television programmes, school competitions and environmental fairs. Workshops have been held for specific target groups such as Members of Parliament and Senate, women's groups, chiefs, the business community, District Development Councils, youth groups, local authorities, etc.

## 3 Scope of the National Action Plan

The Agenda 21 National Action Plan has identified 17 priority areas. It focuses in particular on socio-economic dimensions, management and conservation of natural resources and promotion of community participation, some of which are listed below:

*Socio-Economic Dimensions*

- combating poverty;
- managing demographic dynamics;
- promoting the sustainable development of human settlements; and
- integrating development in decision-making.

*Conservation and Management of Natural Resources*

- integrated land management;
- agriculture and food security;
- promoting sustainable mountain development;
- conservation of biodiversity;
- climate change;
- desertification and drought;
- energy resources;
- combating deforestation; and
- water resources management.

*Getting People Involved*

- empowering women;
- NGOs and the private sector;
- science and technology; and
- promoting education, public awareness and training.

The plan outlines objectives and strategies for each of the programmes and clearly specifies responsibilities to be taken by the different agencies during the implementation process.

## 4 Institutional Arrangements for Implementation

In order to foster coordination and integration of environmental issues in the decision-making process, some new structures are being established:

- Environmental units (EUs) are to be established in line ministries to give advice to their respective ministries and act as focal points for planning and integrating environmental considerations into development projects. These units will also ensure that budgetary allocations adequately cover remedial actions, and will be responsible for the preparation and supervision of the EIA of projects in their ministries, and for liaising with the National Environment Secretariat (NES) for approval of the environmental impact statement. The units will also assist in providing information for preparation of the Annual State of the Environment Report. Regular (monthly) meetings will be scheduled between the NES and the EUs to ensure continuous dialogue and common understanding on various issues.
- A Technical Advisory Committee (TAC) made up from the directors of relevant ministries has already been established to advise the Chief Executive of NES on all issues that will be tabled before the Task Force of Principal Secretaries (TFPS) for approval by the National Environmental Council. This is to build confidence amongst line ministries and ensure that ministries are sufficiently involved in NES activities, and that their mandates are integrated with environmental considerations.
- A non-governmental Environmental Advisory Commission is to be involved in NES activities in order to foster trust between the government and NGOs, and to promote NGO participation in environment related activities.

## 5 Strategies for Implementation

The government acknowledges that if current environmental trends are to be arrested, and sustainable development is to be achieved, new strategies will have to be adopted. The Agenda 21 National Action Plan strives to pursue this through the following strategies:

- public participation and empowerment, ensuring community participation in the planning, execution and management of projects;
- adoption of an integrated approach, where initiatives by various sectors are coordinated and, should be designed to complement and reinforce each other, thereby avoiding duplication;
- promoting research and information exchange to improve understanding and awareness of environmental implications of development;
- establishment of a resource and policy planning framework in order to review the relevance to the Action Plan and to support the formulation of new polices where necessary;
- capacity-building at all levels, including training for the highest professional and the basic technical grades;
- promoting donor coordination and collaboration to avoid duplication of efforts;
- promoting enhanced regional cooperation, recognizing the interconnections of many of Lesotho's environmental

issues with other developments in the region;
- addressing the root causes of poverty and clarifying linkages between poverty and environmental degradation, to assist in policy formulation; and
- monitoring progress, including setting environmental standards and attainment targets in order to monitor progress.

## 6 Legal Framework

A Framework Environmental Management Law is being prepared with UNEP's assistance. Local experts will be responsible for drafting the law, which will be put before Parliament in the first half of 1996. Thereafter sectoral laws will be reviewed to fit into this Framework Law. Wide consultations will be undertaken during the preparatory process, so that the law will gain public support from all sectors of the society, and will be clearly understood at the grassroots level.

## 7 Financial Resources

The government recognizes that, without adequate financial resources and political commitment to the implementation of the Agenda 21 National Action Plan, the cyclical process of environmental degradation and poverty will continue and intensify. It has therefore been recommended that the government set aside a sum equivalent to one per cent of its annual budget for environmental management programmes. In this manner, implementation of programmes will not be affected by budget constraints. It will also be an indication of the government's commitment to addressing environmental problems in the country.

Other supplementary funds will be sought from the following potential sources:

- the donor community;
- UN agencies such as UNDP and UNEP, especially with regard to capacity-building; and
- an environmental fund, which is to be established to specifically target community-based poverty alleviation programmes – contributions for such a fund can be in kind or in cash, and contributions will be sought from donors, the communities themselves, individuals, NGOs and the private and business communities.

## 8 Lessons Learned

### Strengths

A number of strengths can be identified in the process which Lesotho has followed to develop its Agenda 21 National Action Plan. These include:

- high-level political will and commitment;
- location of the NES in the Office of the Prime Minister, which is appropriate and conducive for fostering inter-sectoral coordination;
- building on the foundations of the previous strategy, which had popular support;
- sensitization to environmental issues and an increased awareness and appreciation of the concept of sustainable development;
- integration of the Action Plan with the national development planning process through the NES reviews of sectoral submissions for the five-year development planning process; and
- initiation of policy and legislative changes.

### Weaknesses

Some weaknesses of the Lesotho experience include:

- a largely donor-driven process;
- weakness of the coordinating agency in professional expertise and dependence on external expertise;
- dependence on donor funding that is unsustainable; and
- absence of clear indicators for monitoring success.

*Lessons*

Five major lessons can be identified from the Lesotho experience:

- political will and commitment at the highest level are a prerequisite for the successful implementation of strategies for sustainability;
- community participation and continuous dialogue with all sectors of the civil society in the planning and implementation of sustainable strategies should be an integral part of the development process;
- public awareness campaigns should form the basis of sustainable development goals and should appeal to the traditional, social and cultural values of a given society;
- coordination of plans and strategies for promoting sustainable development requires an effective, technically competent agency with the necessary skills to articulate and interact with different interest groups; and
- capacity-building lies at the centre of sustainable development and so there should be vigorous attempts to give necessary training and skills to those agencies charged with responsibilities for the implementation of strategies for sustainability.

## 9 Chronology

1988    NEAP process initiated, with district consultations.

April: National conference to discuss findings of the consultations.

1989    Finalization of NEAP and its adoption by the government.

1994    Proposal for implementation of the NEAP by the government, with UNDP assistance.

1995    May: One-week workshop to review implementation of NEAP, leading to the commencement of the preparation of an Agenda 21 National Action Plan.

Agenda 21 National Action Plan finalized/approved. Technical Advisory Committee established to advise the Chief Executive of the National Environment Council.

1996    Preparation of a Framework Environmental Management Law.

### Annex 2: Functions of the National Environment Secretariat

- Provision of technical advice in collaboration with line ministries and formulation of policies and programmes which are of importance to the environment and natural resource base of Lesotho.
- Preparation of an Annual State of the Environment Report.
- Preparation of Guidelines for Environment Review Procedures.
- Development of the nation's environmental policy, including reviews of existing legislation.
- Promotion of links with NGOs and the private sector on environmental issues.
- Formulation of multi-sectoral integrated conservation programmes to promote employment, conservation and development.
- Promotion of environmental research, education, training and public awareness.
- Preparation of standards and guidelines for the monitoring of natural resources and environmental quality.
- Resolution of interagency conflicts and national trade-offs in the management of the natural resource base and the maintenance of environmental quality.
- Consultation and coordination with donors, and observance of international commitments and treaty obligations.

# *Malawi*

*National Environmental Action Plan
and Support Programme*

Zipangani Mauru Vokhiwa,
Ministry of Research and
Environmental Affairs

**Estimated population 1992:** 10.2
million; **Land area:** 94,000 km²;
**Ecological zones:** Great Rift Valley, high
plateaus, Shire highlands; **Climate:**
moderate in centre, tropical in south;
**Annual rainfall:** 740mm; **Forest and
woodland area:** 34,000 km²; **GNP per
capita:** US$230; **Main industries:**
agriculture (tobacco, sugar, tea, cotton,
groundnuts and maize), textiles; **ODA
received per capita:** US$47.9;
**Population growth rate** (1992–2000):
2.3 per cent; **Life expectancy at birth:**
45.6 years; **Adult literacy rate:** 53.9 per
cent; **Access to safe water:** 56 per cent;
**Access to health services:** 80 per cent;
**Access to sanitation:** 60 per cent

# 1 Introduction

In the late 1970s the Malawi government became increasingly concerned about the deterioration of the country's environment and the associated economic loss of natural resources. Changing weather patterns and severe droughts in the early 1980s heightened public awareness and concern. This emphasized the need for urgent action to achieve sustainable natural resource conservation and management.

In 1987 a National Committee for the Environment (NCE) was established; a secretariat to service it was created within the Ministry of Forestry and Natural Resources. The NCE was mandated to do the following:

- to ensure that development does not lead to further environmental degradation;
- to arrange for the rehabilitation of degraded land; and
- to advise on policies which the government should adopt to address environmental issues.

In order for the NCE to achieve its objectives, the secretariat had a mandate to coordinate the activities of the various sectors whose activities impact on the environment, to resolve conflicts and to liaise with donors.

Because of the secretariat's coordinating role, it was transferred to the Office of the President and Cabinet (OPC) in 1989. There it was merged with the secretariat for the National Research Council, which was coordinating research activities in the country. This combination was renamed the Department of Research and Environmental Affairs (DREA) in 1991.

With this department in place, Malawi participated in UNCED in June 1992 in Rio de Janeiro, Brazil. Since 1994, DREA has been elevated to ministerial status as the Ministry of Research and Environmental Affairs (MOREA).

In response to the agreements made at UNCED, and in line with government concern to address environmental and natural resource degradation, Malawi started developing a National Environmental Action Plan (NEAP) in late 1992 with assistance from the World Bank. The NEAP process used a participatory approach involving government ministries and departments, NGOs, the private sector, the university, traditional leaders and the local communities. The NEAP document was formally launched in December 1994 by the Vice President of Malawi.

The need for such strategic environmental planning is confirmed by Malawi's new constitution, which was formally adopted in May 1995. In Chapter III, Section 13 (d) there is a commitment to address environmental problems in which the state is required to manage the environment responsibly in order to:

- prevent the degradation of the environment;
- provide a healthy living and working environment for the people of Malawi;
- accord full recognition to the rights of future generations by means of environmental protection; and
- conserve and enhance biological diversity in Malawi.

The NEAP describes the environmental situation existing in the country and identifies nine key environmental issues. It then outlines a series of actions that should be taken in order to redress the accelerating environmental degradation to ensure sustainable utilization and management of natural resources in Malawi. These include necessary policy reform, legislation and possible new investment programmes using a multi-sectoral approach which will be addressed under the NEAP's Environmental Support Programme (ESP).

Task forces, initially 18 in number, but later seven, were formed to address the key environmental concerns. The NEAP further identifies areas where additional action is required to facilitate its implementation. These include:

- clearly defining institutional responsibilities and strengthening capacity;
- formulating guidelines for Environmental Impact Assessments (EIAs) and instituting a mechanism for their implementation; and
- developing a National Environmental Policy (NEP) and an environmental framework law and enacting the law as part of the legislation of the country.

The Malawi NEAP process was intended to be national in scope and comprehensive in content to cover all the principles of sustainable natural resource utilization and management in line with the socio-economic development of the country.

To operationalize the NEAP, the ESP was developed with the overall objective of integrating environmental concerns into the socio-economic development of the country. Through the ESP process it has been possible to identify policies, strategies and priority programmes to address environmental problems.

## 2 Concept and Development

The impetus for the NEAP/ESP came from MOREA (formerly DREA). The World Bank and the Malawi government were both important in developing the concept and initiating the process of establishing an NEAP and the current

ESP. The funds for the preparation of the NEAP/ESP were provided by the World Bank.

*NEAP*

During the preparatory stages of the NEAP 18 task forces were established. Task forces had to determine the current status of the environmental issue for which they were responsible, assess the adequacy of institutional and legal arrangements, and provide a management plan to address the situation. The membership of the task forces was drawn from government, NGOs, the university and the private sector. Through the task forces, 185 people from 51 institutions were involved in the NEAP process.

The 18 issues covered by the task forces, for each of which a paper was prepared, included:

- national context;
- fisheries;
- forestry;
- water resources;
- agriculture;
- energy and mineral resources;
- industry;
- tourism;
- transport and communications;
- health and sanitation;
- land-use planning and management;

- natural hazards;
- population and human settlement;
- biological conservation;
- policies and institutional framework;
- education and public information;
- research; and
- pollution control and waste management.

The task forces took about five months (June to October 1993) to produce their issue papers, which were finalized at a workshop. These reports provided descriptions, analyses and identification of the environmental issues, and recommended remedial actions and project proposals. Following the finalization of the task force reports, eight consultative district workshops, each lasting one week, were held across the country during a three-month period (Malawi has a total of 24 districts; three of them were combined in each workshop). An attempt was made to include grassroots perspectives in the workshops. Consequently, participants included village headmen, church leaders, NGOs, government representatives in the districts and members of women's groups (at least one quarter of the participants were women). Each workshop produced three action plans addressing the environmental problems in each of the districts involved. Poverty was identified during these workshops as one of the key causes of environmental degradation.

From the issue papers and the district workshops nine critical environmental issues were identified. These were:

- soil erosion;
- deforestation;
- water resources degradation;
- depletion of fish stocks;
- threats to biological diversity;
- human habitat degradation;
- high population growth;
- climate change; and
- air pollution.

Prioritization of issues was undertaken by the NEAP secretariat in conjunction with external consultants and was endorsed by the task forces. The NEAP document has two volumes: *Volume 1 – Issue Papers*, and *Volume 2 – District Action Plans*. The compilation of the NEAP took over six months, and was completed in early 1994.

### ESP

While the NEAP was charged with integrating environmental concerns into the socio-economic development of the country, it does not lend itself easily to implementation. Therefore, the ESP was developed as a means of identifying strategies, policies and priority programmes which will translate the NEAP into action.

The development of the ESP involved seven task forces, on:

- soil degradation;
- deforestation;
- water degradation and fisheries;
- loss of biodiversity;
- human habitat degradation and population growth;
- pollution and air quality; and
- microprojects.

The last task force looked mainly at the logistics of incorporating poverty reduction into the ESP activities and the establishment of a fund for use by the grassroots communities to address the environmental issues in their areas. The ESP document has a section on co-management to facilitate the implementation of programmes which cut across several sectors.

The ESP will also address the areas where the NEAP has identified additional action is required to facilitate its implementation. These include:

- clearly defining institutional responsibilities and strengthening capacity;
- formulating guidelines for EIAs and instituting a mechanism for implementation; and
- developing an NEP and an environmental framework law and enacting the law as part of the country's legislation.

All three of these activities are now at an advanced stage of development.

ESP work on the different task force areas includes sub-programmes in the following areas:

- environmental policy and institutional development;
- institutional development focusing on institutional capacity-building, training, institution and infrastructure development, and human resources development;
- promotion of local participation in environmental management;
- priority environmental programmes and investment projects; and
- community environment microproject fund (CEMF) and co-management of natural resources.

Although detailed ESP sub-programme activity outlines have been completed and the donor community has been briefed, costing of these sub-programmes has not yet been completed. Once finalized, the ESP programme will be circulated to various interested parties, including the donors, to solicit funding for the various programme components.

Using participatory approaches, communities will develop their own environment-related activities which will be funded by the CEMF. This fund will serve to empower the local communities.

Additionally, this component will enshrine a community/collaborative management of natural resources whereby local communities and line ministries and sectors will develop projects for collaborative management of natural resources.

## 3 Relationship to Development Planning

The Ministry of Economic Planning and Development (EP&D) is responsible for formulating and approving economic and social development plans as well as monitoring implementation. The Ministry of Research and Environmental Affairs (MOREA) is mandated to coordinate all the environmental issues in development planning in the country. The NEAP/ESP secretariat is housed in MOREA. From 1 July 1995 it has been incorporated within the ministry structure in the Environmental Management Unit. This unit is charged with the coordination of NEAP/ESP activities, while line agencies and other stakeholders are the implementing agents. Development projects formulated under the ESP, together with all the relevant proposals from line ministries and other agencies, are submitted by MOREA to EP&D for appraisal and funding within the Public Sector Investment Programme (PSIP). As a result, there is a close and good relationship between MOREA and EP&D.

The NEAP/ESP process is currently being integrated into the development planning system beginning the 1995/96 fiscal year. One aspect of this is the identification of focal points within institutions, as a means of facilitating the coordination of environmental issues in the country. The focal point is either a department or a person, depending on the institution. These people form a network in which the EP&D and MOREA staff are central.

The creation of MOREA led to some resentment in other sectoral ministries who felt that no line ministry should coordinate the environmental affairs of another ministry. However, MOREA is making efforts to ensure that implementation of all the investment projects under the ESP and other environmental issues are implemented by the relevant and appropriate line agencies in the various ministries, departments, NGOs and the private sector, and not by itself. The situation will be clarified soon, once the Environmental Management Bill is passed.

It is expected that local communities will develop projects at their level which will be funded by a CEMF. Steps are underway to form an Environment Endowment Fund to fund these projects.

In summary, the division of responsibilities with respect to NEAP/ESP and the environment is as follows:

*MOREA*

- coordinate the ESP as a secretary to the NCE and the Technical Consultative Group on Environment (TCGE), the national technical advisory body to the NCE;
- be in charge of those projects where MOREA itself is the implementing institution;
- provide necessary support to line ministries and agencies to enable them to fulfil their environmental obligations, including policy guidelines and training;
- manage the CEMF;
- act as a reporting and coordinating agency between the various implementing agencies and the donor community; and
- establish a monitoring system by collating information from the different implementing agencies to provide a picture of the changes taking place.

*Implementing Agencies*

- formulate their own policies and administrative guidelines on environmental management within their jurisdiction;
- identify in-house training requirements and implement environmental training and other environmental activities in support of ongoing projects; and
- implement new environmental investment projects.

*Local Communities*

- identify and prepare community environmental micro-projects; and
- implement the locally planned projects with financial assistance from the CEMF.

## 4 Lessons Learned

The main factors favouring the NEAP/ ESP strategy were:

- the involvement of key individuals within various line ministries and agencies, NGOs, the university and other parastatals, the private sector and the full participation of the local communities at district level;
- the willingness of the World Bank to fund the initial workshop consultative meetings and workshops, the establishment of an NEAP secretarial unit from 1993 to June 1995 and finally the establishment and support of the ESP; and
- the willingness of most donor agencies to channel their environmental support to the Malawi Government through MOREA's ESP unit.

The main factors hindering the strategy include:

- lack of locally-based financial resources which would have allowed the immediate implementation of some of the planned activities instead of waiting for donor funding for all of the proposed initiatives – local communities therefore question whether the NEAP exercise, in which they participated fully, was real or just another government 'gimmick';
- lack of trained personnel in both MOREA and the line ministries, which will delay the implementation process (during which time the deterioration of the natural resource base continues);
- harmonizing of the sectoral policies and the National Environmental Policy will require liaison and education between MOREA and the implementing line ministries and agencies; and
- uncertainty over the ESP, due to the absence of a government pledge to set aside sufficient financial resources to finance the ESP during the first five-year phase and the subsequent remaining 15-year strategy.

5    *Chronology*

1964    Independence from the British government for Nyasaland (under the Federation of Southern Rhodesia and Nyasaland).

1966    Malawi a republic; agriculture becomes the backbone of the country's economy leading to the opening up of more land for crop and livestock production.

1976    Environmental Training Unit established in the Ministry of Forestry and Natural Resources.

1982    The National Committee for the Environment (NCE) established, a high-level body on the environment.

1991    Environmental unit elevated to Department of Research and Environmental Affairs (DREA) after merger with the National Research Council of Malawi. DREA is placed under the Office of the President and Cabinet (OPC).

1992    Malawi attends the 'Earth Summit' in Rio de Janeiro, Brazil. Malawi starts an NEAP programme with assistance from the World Bank using a participatory and multi-sectoral approach.

1993    NEAP Secretariat established including three World Bank consultants, an NEAP Coordinator, an environmentalist and an economist.

1994    June: Malawi attains a multi-party democracy after a 30-year one-party rule.

        December: NEAP launched by the Vice President. ESP preparation starts.

1995    March: Parliamentary Advisory Committee on Environment established by Cabinet. Environmental impact assessment (EIA) guidelines and procedures drafted and discussed at a national workshop in Blantyre.

        May: Draft National Environmental Policy discussed at a national workshop and finalized in August 1995.

        June: Draft Environmental Management Bill discussed at a national workshop and submitted to Parliament for enactment.

        NEAP/ESP secretariat, funded by the World Bank, concludes and hands over its responsibility to MOREA after programme document submission to the World Bank for review.

# Nigeria

*National Conservation Strategy and
National Environmental Action Plan*

AYODELE A OLOJEDE, FEDERAL
ENVIRONMENTAL PROTECTION AGENCY;
AND A R K SABA, NATURAL RESOURCES
CONSERVATION COUNCIL

**Estimated population 1992:** 102.1
million; **Land area:** 911,000 km²;
**Ecological zones:** coastal mangroves,
tropical forest strip, open woodland and
savannah plains, bordering on the Sahara
Desert; **Climate:** two rainy seasons in
coastal areas, dry season in the north,
October–April; **Annual rainfall:** 4,000
mm in the south and 750 mm in the
north; **Forest and woodland area:**
113,000 km²; **GNP per capita:** US$330;
**Main industries:** agriculture, oil and gas
production, mining; **ODA received per
capita:** US$2.00; **Population growth
rate (1992–2000):** 2.9 per cent; **Life
expectancy at birth:** 50.4 years; **Adult
literacy rate:** 52.5 per cent; **Access to safe
water:** 36 per cent; **Access to health
services:** 66 per cent; **Access to
sanitation:** 35 per cent

## 1 Introduction

Nigeria's strategy consists of two independently-developed initiatives. The first, the NCS, was prepared almost entirely by Nigerians, in a process led by Nigerians, was approved in 1988 and is currently being implemented. The second, an NEAP document, was prepared by the World Bank with Nigerian participation in a process led by the World Bank. Work on an NEAP report started in 1988 and was completed in 1990; the report is now being implemented.

The focus of the NCS is largely on conservation of natural resources and biodiversity while that of the NEAP is largely the control of pollution and land degradation. The NCS has been poorly coordinated with the development planning process, whereas the NEAP has better links with development planning but virtually ignores the NCS.

The NCS has led to the establishment of additional conservation agencies, the adoption of a forest policy goal to increase the forest estate from 10 to 20 per cent of the country's land area, and the compilation of basic information on Nigeria's biodiversity. It is seriously underfunded, however. On the other hand, the NEAP had led to the strengthening of the Federal Environmental Protection Agency (FEPA) by subsuming the Natural Resources Conservation Council (NRCC), a body established to oversee implementation of NCS. The agency has also been placed under the Presidency with an expanded mandate covering all natural resource conservation issues.

Neither the NCS nor the NEAP were developed with sufficient participation. It would have been better to have developed the NEAP, not as an independent initiative, but by building on the locally-developed NCS. The NEAP has substantially greater influence on international assistance than the NCS, but assistance continues to be poorly coordinated and non-strategic. Both the NCS and NEAP would be greatly strengthened by developing them further as a single strategy.

Under the provision of the NEAP loan agreement, NRCC will undertake a review of the NCS. This would provide an opportunity to integrate the NEAP and the NCS, and possibly transform them into a more comprehensive National Sustainable Development Strategy which could serve as an umbrella for the many existing and proposed thematic, regional or eco-geographical strategies. These include the National Forestry Plan, the National Waste Management Strategy, the Drought and Desertification Control Plan, and the National Water Resources Master Plan. Others under preparation include the State-level Environmental Action Plans (SEAPs), and the Coastal Zone Management Action Plan.

NRCC and FEPA, together with some related agencies in the Federal Ministry of Agriculture, are being merged into a single institution whose structure will follow that of the NRCC. This could also facilitate the development of a single strategy.

## 2 Scope and Objectives

### NCS

The NCS focuses on conservation of Nigeria's main renewable resources, including vegetation and forage, water, fisheries and other marine resources, wild animals, and soil. The overall objective of the NCS is to provide development planning with a long-term, strategic approach to the management of natural resources and their uses. Specific objectives are:

- maintenance of genetic diversity to ensure permanence in the supply of materials to satisfy basic human needs and improve the well-being of society;
- protection of the environment, eg protection of catchment areas to enhance water resources and check soil erosion, protection of grazing lands against desert encroachment, and the stabilization of coastal environments;
- regulation of environmental balances in relation to such factors as carbon dioxide emission levels and bio-geochemical cycles;

- maintaining the scientific value of natural ecosystems, the study of which is required to enhance conservation, to improve the management of human systems, and to provide clues to technical innovations in agriculture, medicine and industry; and
- enhancing the amenity value of natural resources, including aesthetic, heritage, religious, sentimental, ethical and recreational values on which tourism may be built.

### NEAP

Preparation of the NEAP began with an assessment of Nigeria's environmental problems and of the interdependence of environmental concerns and the economy in Nigeria. The objectives of the assessment were to:

- carry out a geophysical assessment of the environmental quality of various ecological zones;
- identify the key environmental concerns and assess their probable causes, both direct and indirect;
- examine the substantive provisions of existing legislation, federal, state and regional policies and institutions that focus specifically on environmental issues;
- assess the impact of economic policies on the environment; and
- examine the options available to redress environmental degradation.

## 3 Relationship to Development Planning

The main focus of the NCS document is on conservation of natural resources. The NCS attempts to commit agencies at different levels to integrate conservation and development at every stage, calling for cross-sectoral conservation measures within national development plans, and for ecological impact studies at the conceptual stage of development projects. The Ministry of National Planning (replaced in 1992 by the National Planning Commission) was not, however, involved significantly in preparing the NCS document, which was essentially done in parallel to the development planning process.

Responsibilities for management and use of renewable resources fall primarily on local and state governments. Although the NCS document suggests a coordinated approach to resource conservation, providing guidance and proposing standards for integrating conservation and development, only now are local and state governments becoming involved in the strategy.

In contrast, the main focus of the NEAP report was expressly on the linkages between environmental concerns and economic issues. An effort was made to assess the economic losses to Nigeria if environmental degradation continues, and to demonstrate the relationship between economic considerations and environ-

mental quality. There was also a strong emphasis on institutional aspects. The report was published after formal discussions involving the Ministry of National Planning. However, leadership did not come from that Ministry but from the World Bank.

## 4 Initial Development

### NCS

The inspiration to prepare the NCS came from the World Conservation Strategy (WCS) when it was launched in March 1980. The WCS urged every country to undertake its own strategy to focus attention on relevant priority requirements for conservation and to provide a way to coordinate the efforts of government agencies and NGOs to implement its recommendations. The WCS helped catalyze implementation of the 1968 Organization of African Unity (OAU) African Convention for the Conservation of Nature and Natural Resources, to which Nigeria is a signatory. Parties to this treaty undertake to adopt measures necessary for conservation, use and development of soil, water, floral and faunal resources in accordance with scientific principles and with due regard for the best interests of the people.

Nigeria's NCS was therefore developed to address issues of renewable resource conservation with the aim of guaranteeing sustainable benefits to the greatest number of citizens. It is the product of three years' work by governmental and non-governmental agencies jointly coordinated by the Federal Department of Forestry (a government agency) and the Nigerian Conservation Foundation (an NGO).

Work on the NCS began in 1983 at a meeting of two policy advisory bodies, the National Wildlife Conservation Committee and the National Forestry Development Committee. The meeting proposed a thorough review of the status of conservation in Nigeria. A two-day national seminar in February 1985 assembled for the first time in Nigeria more than 100 scientists, technical experts, administrators and resource managers to discuss strategies for the conservation of fresh water, fisheries, the sea, soil, wildlife, forests and grazing lands, and assess the economic and financial implications of conservation programmes in Nigeria.

In 1985 and 1986, a drafting committee led by A R K Saba prepared the NCS document. Other key players included directors from the Federal Department of Fisheries, National Institute of Oceanography and Marine Research, Federal Department of Water Resources, Federal Department of Agricultural Land Resources, Forestry Research Institute of Nigeria, and researchers and academicians from universities, research institutes, and UNESCO's Regional Office for Science

and Technology in Africa (Dakar). The drafting committee did the following:

- summarized information generated at the seminar on the status of each of the renewable resources and threats to their conservation;
- integrated this information with suggestions received from a cross-section of Nigerian society, following a process of formal consultations;
- identified specific actions required for the inventory and evaluation of vegetation and forage, water, marine and fisheries, wildlife and soil resources;
- determined the actions required to enhance efficient use of natural resources;
- proposed ways and means of organizing and carrying out intensive public enlightenment programmes; and
- set out administrative and legislative measures including the creation of coordinating machinery and capacity-building through training and research.

The financial implications of implementing the NCS were not addressed. The National Council of Ministers approved the NCS in February 1988; the NRCC was set up in 1989 to oversee its implementation. This body merged with FEPA in 1992.

*NEAP*

A year after approval of the NCS, the government of Nigeria requested the assistance of the World Bank to define environmental priorities and assess the type and scope of reform required to redress environmental degradation.

The World Bank prepared a literature review and draft assessment analyzing the linkages between environmental concerns and economic issues. This was followed by a World Bank environmental mission, which included Nigerian experts. The mission visited nine of the 21 states (existing at the time) to assess the extent of environmental degradation, surveyed environmental organizations at the state level to assess their capacity to fulfil their responsibilities, and reviewed legislation and institutional arrangements to deal with environmental concerns, including overlaps and conflicts among key environmental agencies. The mission commissioned 20 sectoral reports by Nigerian experts.

Based on its findings and on other Nigerian and foreign contributions, the Bank prepared the draft report 'Towards Developing an Environmental Action Plan for Nigeria'. This was discussed at three workshops in Nigeria. Participants included officials of federal and state governments, experts, members of NGOs, the private sector, and academia. After internal reviews within the Bank, the report was formally transmitted to the government for review by policy-makers. Formal discussions were held in

November 1990. In May 1991, the Ministry of Budget and Planning hosted a national environmental workshop in collaboration with FEPA to discuss the issues raised in the report. Nigeria and the World Bank signed a loan agreement in 1991 for the preparation of the NEAP.

*The NCS/NEAP relationship*

The initial invitation to the World Bank came from the Finance Ministry and FEPA. The opportunity for FEPA to work closely with NRCC and for the NEAP to build on the NCS (with its important characteristics as a local effort) was missed. Instead the NEAP became characterized as FEPA's interest, as the NCS was NRCC's interest, and the importance of the NCS was downplayed. The World Bank's report suggested there was an overlap between the two agencies, although their mandates are distinct. NRCC's responsibility was the 'green' agenda: conservation of nature and natural resources. FEPA's responsibility is the 'brown' agenda: pollution control. The NEAP report is largely concerned with pollution and land degradation, and much less so with biodiversity or renewable resources. The loan agreement signed in 1991 contains only a small provision for the NCS.

The issues of overlap and coordination were decisively resolved with the merger of NRCC with FEPA in 1992 through a FEPA Amendment Decree which nullified the NRCC Decree. FEPA now oversees the implementation of NCS and is undertaking a review, with the ultimate purpose of having an umbrella sustainable development strategy. The merger of NRCC with FEPA is intended to ensure coordination and integration of related activities.

As well as the Federal Ministry of Finance, which is the coordinating agency, five different agencies are involved in implementing the NEAP: the Ecological Funds Office, the Federal Department of Agricultural Land Resources, the Federal Department of Forestry, the Federal Ministry of Water Resources, and FEPA.

## 5 Implementation and Results

### NCS

A major step in the implementation of the NCS was the establishment of the NRCC in 1989, mandated to oversee the implementation of the NCS. It had sufficient powers to approve the implementation of any of the actions specified in the NCS document. As the apex organization for natural resource conservation in Nigeria, it also had the mandate to coordinate conservation of natural resources, formulate a national conservation policy in line with the NCS, and monitor the activities of the various conservation agencies in the country. The Council was also mandated to resolve any

conflicts among these agencies, designate sites and species of conservation interest, grant honours and give awards for projects that enhance national conservation objectives, and take fiscal measures to encourage conservation of natural resources in Nigeria. It was to provide grants for scientific investigations and studies of the ecological impacts of projects, and, in collaboration with other bodies, control coastal zone development to minimize erosion of the coastline.

Implementation of the NCS has also included:

- preparation of a national policy for natural resources conservation;
- formulation of a National Forest Policy which focuses on increasing the forest estate from 10 per cent to 20 per cent of the total land area of the country;
- establishment of a National Centre for Genetic Resources and Biotechnology;
- establishment of National Parks Governing Board; and
- compilation of annotated checklists of the wild plants and animals of Nigeria (the checklist of wild plants covers more than 7,000 species, providing information on distribution, ecology, phenology and probable uses of each).

### NEAP

Implementation of the NEAP started in late 1992 with institutional reforms, a development which was given impetus by UNCED at Rio. The promulgation of the FEPA Amendment Decree in December 1992 set in train a process of merging environment related units, including NRCC and units situated in line ministries, into FEPA. In addition to its purely regulatory function before the reform, FEPA's mandate was expanded to cover soil erosion, desertification control and natural resource conservation.

Implementing the Amendment Decree, which did not commence until 1993, was initially problematic as it involved the merger of disparate environmental units with conflicting perspectives and goals. This led to a crisis of leadership as well as mutual suspicion and recriminations among staff. However, decisive intervention at the policy level and strong leadership led to a quick return to normality.

A key advantage which the NEAP has over the NCS in terms of implementation is its full integration into the national rolling plans and the annual budgetary provision for implementation. Most of the local costs, including infrastructural support, personnel costs and training are directly borne by the government, while costs for overseas training, consultancies and equipment are mainly donor funded.

At present the NEAP is in a cyclical process of development and implementation with feedback from the experience of

implementation contributing to the development of the NEAP. There are four major areas where implementation is ongoing:

- supporting the development of the states' environmental action plans;
- development of environmental baseline studies;
- undertaking institutional and capacity-building; and
- developing an environmental data bank and information management system.

The latter three of these activities are components of an Environmental Management Project which is funded through a World Bank loan agreement.

*Participation*

Although both the NCS and the NEAP appear to have involved various stakeholders during the development and implementation phases, the nature of participation appears cosmetic as many of the recommendations were not products of a consensus. The government and its agencies also appear to have played a dominant role in both strategies, a reflection of the fact that these strategies evolved under military regimes which could only permit limited participation.

For example, the institutional reforms arising from the implementation of the NEAP and NCS did not reflect the views

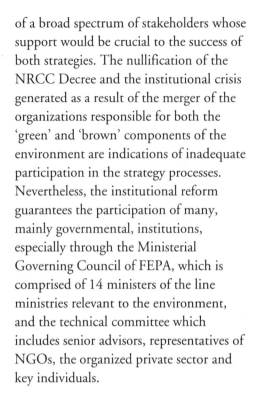

of a broad spectrum of stakeholders whose support would be crucial to the success of both strategies. The nullification of the NRCC Decree and the institutional crisis generated as a result of the merger of the organizations responsible for both the 'green' and 'brown' components of the environment are indications of inadequate participation in the strategy processes. Nevertheless, the institutional reform guarantees the participation of many, mainly governmental, institutions, especially through the Ministerial Governing Council of FEPA, which is comprised of 14 ministers of the line ministries relevant to the environment, and the technical committee which includes senior advisors, representatives of NGOs, the organized private sector and key individuals.

### *Monitoring and Evaluation*

For both the NCS and the NEAP, the monitoring and assessment mechanisms are generally inadequate. However, the guidelines and standards already put in place by FEPA would assist in measuring performance. A Department of Planning and Evaluation has also been created within the Agency and it has responsibility for measuring performance against targets. Similarly, the Department of Inspectorate and Compliance Monitoring are to ensure compliance with industrial standards already approved by the government.

## 6 *Factors Favouring the Strategy*

### *NCS*

The success so far with implementation has been due to the following factors:

- the government's firm commitment to international conservation treaties, such as the OAU's African Convention on Conservation of Nature and Natural Resources, the World Heritage Convention, the Convention on International Trade in Endangered Species (CITES), the Convention on Migratory Species, and the 1992 Biodiversity Convention;
- the launching of the WCS, because it showed the country how each nation could achieve sustainable development;
- consistent pressure on government by conservation NGOs, such as the Nigerian Conservation Foundation and the Nigerian Environmental Study/ Action Team;
- the persuasive approach of conservationists within the public service on the principles of sustainable development; and
- the encouragement of policy makers who provided the necessary financial support and legislation.

International assistance has been important for implementation: the FAO provided technical assistance for the preparation of a national policy for conservation and is supporting a wood residue utilization and charcoal production project; the World Bank has funded a forestry project, among others; the African Development Bank has funded a plantation programme; the European Union is funding arid zone afforestation; the Overseas Development Administration of the United Kingdom has funded part of Nigeria's Tropical Forestry Action Plan and a forestry project in Cross River State; and a number of bilateral and non-governmental agencies are supporting conservation projects, such as the Cross River National Park and the Hadejia-Nuguru Wetlands Conservation Project. Welcome though this support is, implementation of the NCS requires international investment of a much higher level and careful strategic coordination of these various initiatives.

### NEAP

Unlike the NCS, the NEAP contains a quantifiable statement of objectives, has a substantial financial support base and is fully integrated into the macro-economic plans of the government. Government interest in the Action Plan was sustained by the unrelenting pressures from the World Bank who felt concerned about its past activities in the country which had led to serious environmental degradation. The international attention given to global environmental and sustainable development in the last few years further compelled the government to focus on developing the NEAP. The favourable terms of the World Bank loans for environmental management, with their long repayment period and low interest rate, also encouraged the government's active role in the preparation of the strategy. The strong personality of FEPA's Chief Executive and the agency's location in the Presidency are also relevant factors that favoured the strategy.

## 7 Factors Hindering the Strategy

### NCS

Inadequate financing has been a problem since work on the NCS began. Implementation was also seriously delayed: approval of the NCS came almost two years after the document was completed, and another three years elapsed after approval before implementation began. Continuing problems include:

- frequent changes of personnel at policy levels;
- a weak database constraining policy formulation, project planning and implementation, and funding for research and data gathering has remained very low;
- poor enforcement of existing rules and regulations, including wanton disregard for laws against poaching wild animals, bush burning, and regulations on

timber felling, fishing and mine reclamation;

- alienation of local people due to overemphasis on prohibitions rather than on encouraging local participation in conservation programmes;
- personnel constraints, especially in extension services;
- limited perception of conservation benefits at the grassroots level; and
- the NRCC–FEPA merger.

*NEAP*

The NEAP is essentially a donor-driven strategy which is mainly focused on non-tangible issues, data management, policy and institutional reforms and studies. It pays much less attention to biodiversity or renewable resources. Apart from being donor-driven, there are other factors that tend to hinder the strategy. These include:

- treating environmental issues as mere political issues which provide an avenue to receive international support but without necessarily providing the local financial base;
- political uncertainties and general economic downturn;
- institutional and leadership crises arising from institutional reforms and creating delays in strategy implementation;
- not incorporating monitoring and evaluation mechanisms;
- guided and limited participation of stakeholders;

- placing emphasis on non-tangible issues rather than environmental issues;
- failure to build on previous experience of strategy implementation;
- not incorporating poverty-alleviating objectives into the strategy; and
- a poor data base.

## 8 Lessons Learned

The NCS has been a completely Nigerian initiative. Apart from some help provided by UNESCO's Regional Office for Science and Technology in Africa (Dakar), the NCS document was prepared entirely by Nigerian organizations and individuals. In contrast, the NEAP process was led by the World Bank, although Nigerians participated. However, the most important lessons of the relationship between the NCS and NEAP are that:

- international initiatives should build on local initiatives. The NEAP should have been clearly seen as building on the NCS as part of a single strategy for Nigeria;
- a major contribution that international and other external agencies can make is to coordinate their assistance and ensure that it is in line with the strategy. If the strategy is insufficiently developed to provide adequate guidance, assistance could be given to make it so. Large inappropriate loans that do not reflect the strategy are still a

problem for Nigeria; and

- wide participation and national leadership are necessary for the strategy to last. No public meeting was held to build public support for the NCS.

Policy formulation was not a part of the NCS document. As a result, despite the establishment of NRCC under the chairmanship of the President, the NCS did not have a clear place in government policy. The lack of a clearly defined policy meant that conservation programmes were difficult to implement. It also left a vacuum, leading to problems between the NCS and the NEAP.

Institutional reforms are not necessarily a panacea for successful environmental and sustainable development programmes unless there is a clear demonstration that alternative institutions proposed are substantially more beneficial than the existing ones. Even then, the reform must be carried out in a democratic and participatory manner in order to avoid internal organizational turbulence.

Furthermore, an institutional structure devoted to the environment requires a very strong and influential individual who will help to sustain the efficiency and effectiveness of the organization. An individual without the requisite personality, although professionally qualified, may not be able to influence policy decisions in favour of sustainable development. Consequently, apart from being an influential and strong personality, the administrator of an environmental agency should be at least of Cabinet rank.

The comparative advantage of home-grown and country-driven initiatives as opposed to donor-driven efforts would have to be determined in the future after drawing more lessons from the current experience. If the present indicators are reliable, however, we can infer that donor-driven strategies, despite being the best means of securing funding, tend to be highly capitalized, internationally priced, and therefore costly. They also embrace objectives that are sometimes difficult to internalize or wrongly prioritized.

Finally, strategy formulation and implementation should be based on sound and reliable data, be low-input oriented, flexible and comprehensive enough to be able to withstand policy and political changes, encourage community participation, provide allowance for poverty-alleviating measures, and improve job security. Environmental strategies and action plans should not be ends in themselves but the means to achieving sustainable development. Successful implementation requires concerted efforts, collective will and determination, transparency and commitment of internally generated resources, and an assurance of international funding.

## 9 *Chronology*

| | |
|---|---|
| 1983 | Meeting of the National Wildlife Conservation Committee and the National Forestry Development Committee on NCS. |
| 1985 | February: national seminar on NCS, Kano. |
| 1986 | February–September: drafting committee prepares NCS document. |
| 1988 | February: National Council of Ministers approves the NCS. |
| | Establishment of the Federal Environmental Protection Agency (FEPA). |
| 1989 | Establishment of the Natural Resources Conservation Council (NRCC). |
| 1990 | March: World Bank environmental mission. |
| | November: formal discussions between the government of Nigeria and the World Bank on NEAP report. |
| 1991 | Nigeria and the World Bank sign loan agreement. |
| 1992 | Establishment of National Parks Governing Board. |
| | FEPA restructured with an expanded mandate and subsumed NRCC. |

# Serengeti

*Serengeti Regional Conservation Strategy*

JOHN L HOUGH

**Land area:** 30,000 km²; **Physical characteristics:** plains region dominated by grasslands, north characterized by rolling wooded savannah, east dominated by Ngorongoro massif; **Climate:** wet season November–December and February–April; **Annual rainfall:** 400–1200 mm; **Status:** mosaic of national parks, wildlife reserves and communally owned lands, with some private lands, spanning the Kenya–Tanzania border; **Major ethnic groups:** Maasai, Kuria, Sukuma, Datoga, Ikoma, Isenye, Chagga; **Wildlife:** wildebeests, gazelle, zebra, impala, buffalo, lion, leopard, cheetah, wild dog, 200 species of birds; **Major problems:** land-use conflicts, poaching

# 1 Introduction

The Serengeti region comprises those parts of Tanzania and Kenya currently occupied by the Serengeti–Mara migratory ecosystem and its surroundings. It is one of the most important wildlife areas in the world.

The Serengeti Regional Conservation Strategy (SRCS) is being undertaken to integrate resource conservation, and the Serengeti protected area network, into regional development. Long-term conservation is to be achieved through the collaboration of all resource users and managers in adaptive planning and management. At present, the strategy covers only the Tanzanian portion of the ecosystem and involves only the authorities of Tanzania. It is hoped that the strategy will extend to Kenya.

Information assembly and analysis, policy formulation and action planning are occurring at the same time as implementation. Various planning documents have been produced, including a Phase II report and Phase III action plan '*A Plan for Conservation and Development in the Serengeti Region*'. The concept of the strategy has been approved by the Minister for Tourism, Natural Resources and the Environment (MTNRE), a steering committee has been established, and a number of actions are being undertaken. For example, five village authorities have been helped to gain title to their land to ensure that land essential for the Maasai pastoralist way of life is not taken over by outside commercial crop producers.

The strategy documents have not clearly and consistently defined a policy framework, however, and the actions do not yet make up a coherent strategy. In addition, the communities affected by the strategy have no means of participating in decisions about its objectives or how they should be achieved.

# 2 Scope and Objectives

The strategy addresses the full range of human and ecological processes within the Serengeti region from the perspective of long-term conservation of the Serengeti–Mara migratory ecosystem. It is particularly concerned with:

- policy, planning and management of the region's protected areas;
- integrating the protected areas and natural resource conservation activities into the economy of the region;
- the progress of human development and its transition towards sustainability; and
- conflicts between conservation and development objectives and activities.

The goals and objectives of the SRCS have evolved since the strategy's inception in 1985. The current goal is:

- to provide a framework for the integration of the protected area network and resource conservation into regional development so that human development needs and natural resource conservation requirements are reconciled with one another and the long-term conservation of the Serengeti–Mara ecosystem is assured.

The objectives are as follows:

- to conserve the essential natural values of the Serengeti–Mara ecosystem;
- to fulfil the legitimate development needs of the local people; and
- to reconcile and integrate conservation and development objectives and activities so that each can be promoted without detriment to the other.

## 3 Relationship to Development Planning

Within the Tanzanian portion of the ecosystem there are four principal sets of authorities: a central government division, parastatal organizations, regional administrations, and district councils. The SRCS has no executive authority; instead, it involves the national, parastatal and regional organizations through a steering

committee. District councils are not represented on the steering committee.

The Wildlife Division of MTNRE, headed by a director, has executive responsibility for all wildlife outside the statutory protected areas. In addition, he or she has direct responsibility for the Maswa Game Reserve within the Serengeti–Mara ecosystem.

Serengeti National Park is one of 12 national parks, each headed by a warden, administered by the Tanzania National Parks (TANAPA), headed by a director general who is responsible to a board of trustees. Trustees are appointed by the Minister of MTNRE under the National Parks Ordinance. The chair of the board and the director general are appointed by the President.

Ngorongoro Conservation Area is administered by the Ngorongoro Conservation Area Authority, a board appointed by the Minister of MTNRE, to whom the conservator is responsible. Both the chair of the board and the conservator are appointed by the President.

Regional administrations are led by a regional development director who reports to the regional commissioner. The director is advised by regional planning officers, agriculture and livestock officers, natural resources officers and others. Plans and recommendations from the District level are commented on and approved at the regional level before going on to national offices.

District councils are elected through a system of ward councillors. District officers report through the district executive director to the district council. District officers make and act on recommendations of the district councils. They are supported technically by their regional and national offices and are directly responsible for the implementation of conservation and development activities outside the statutory national parks and game reserves.

## 4 Initial Development

The impetus for the strategy came from the Tanzania MTNRE (then called the Ministry of Natural Resources and Tourism). The World Conservation Union (IUCN), the Frankfurt Zoological Society (FZS), TANAPA, and the Serengeti Wildlife Research Institute (SWRI) were all important in developing the concept and initiating the process.

The SRCS was initiated in 1985 at a workshop held at Seronera in the Serengeti National Park. It is a project of the MTNRE in collaboration with IUCN. Following the initial workshop during phase I, work in phase II of the strategy has:

- developed an understanding of the region's resource base, present resource use and constraints to sustainable use;
- identified priority areas for intervention to ensure the effective management of the region's protected areas;
- established the principal reasons for current unsustainable land-use practices;
- developed a variety of pilot activities aimed at improving interactions between the protected areas and the local communities;
- collected wildlife and district infrastructure data to initiate a planning and monitoring process; and
- promoted and enlisted support for the SRCS among regional and national authorities.

Phase III of the Strategy currently encompasses the following:

- developing a regional conservation and development information system for planning and monitoring;
- helping to ensure the conservation and effective management of the protected areas through attracting financial support;
- supporting and implementing pilot activities to improve and stabilize resource use and enhance the economic well-being of local communities; and
- implementing a variety of activities aimed at improving relations between protected areas and local communities.

The Norwegian Agency for International Development (NORAD) provided the money to launch the strategy at the Seronera workshop, and supported the major part of the phase II and phase III work. The European Community Food Aid Counterpart Fund and the FZS also provided essential financial support for phase II.

The chair of the steering committee, currently the Director of Wildlife, is appointed by and represents the Minister of MTNRE. Members are the National Commissioner for Agriculture and Livestock Development, the Director of the National Land-use Planning Commission, the Director of the National Environment Management Council, the Director General of TANAPA, the Conservator of Ngorongoro Conservation Area, the Chief Park Warden of Serengeti National Park, the four regional planning officers, and the regional representatives of the FZS and IUCN's Eastern Africa Regional Office.

The steering committee meets every six months to approve work plans and to discuss and resolve policy issues. The secretary to the steering committee is the SRCS project director, an employee of the Wildlife Division seconded to the SRCS. He is aided by a chief technical advisor who is provided by IUCN.

The project director is responsible for preparing, implementing and monitoring strategy documents. He heads a two-person planning and coordination unit. This unit is supported by a wildlife unit, comprised of two wildlife specialists and a sustainable development (district support) unit, consisting of a land-use planner. Two economists and two sociologists were brought onto the strategy team during phase III.

Phase I of the Strategy, the Seronera workshop, was developed primarily by IUCN at the request of the MTNRE. Phase II was designed by the phase I workshop, implemented by a MTNRE project director and supported by an IUCN technical advisor. The phase II report and phase III planning documents were prepared for the MTNRE by the IUCN Eastern Africa Regional Office based on information supplied by the SRCS secretariat. Planning documents and papers are prepared by the project director and various consultants, often with support from the IUCN regional office. Two planning documents have been produced: '*Toward a Regional Conservation Strategy for the Serengeti*' (MTNRE, Dar-es-Salaam, 1986) and '*Serengeti Regional Conservation Strategy: A Plan for Conservation and Development in the Serengeti Region*' (MTNRE, Dar-es-Salaam, 1991).

A conservation and development information system is being designed to provide information about, and allow formal feedback on, the status and trends of ecological and social indicators within the ecosystem. Formal participation is achieved primarily through the steering committee. No structures exist for participation at district and village levels. Various district and village workshops, on topics like game reserve management plans, village land-use plans and wildlife utilization plans, are held on an *ad hoc* basis in association with SRCS local level planning. Other than that, participation by district officers, elected officials, NGOs, and local communities is informal.

## 5 *Implementation and Results*

Pilot projects and experiments in wildlife use, land tenure allocation and village physical planning have been carried out by the SRCS staff. For example, six different series of hunting experiments have been carried out in Serengeti and Bunda districts to determine and test appropriate village hunting methods. Ground and aerial surveys of wildlife numbers and settlement patterns are conducted regularly as a basis for hunting quotas and planning development. Village boundaries have been surveyed in 17 villages in Loliondo and Salei Divisions, Ngorongoro District; and village authorities helped gain land title for five village areas in Loliondo Division. This has significantly reduced land alienation to outside commercial farming interests, and is seen as crucial to retaining Maasai pastoralist autonomy and way of life in this area.

Support for village development activities is provided through the appropriate district officials. For example, the SRCS is supporting forestry activities in four districts by providing plastic tubing and seeds, spare parts, transport, and bridging funds.

Planning assistance was also provided to the Serengeti National Park Authority to prepare its 1991–1995 management plan; and four vehicles have been acquired for the Serengeti National Park Extension and Tourism Departments.

Planned activities include:

- redistribution of a percentage of the gross revenues of Serengeti National Park and the game reserves to contiguous districts (it is expected that the money will go into district wildlife funds to support village development projects);
- support for tree nurseries and agroforestry;
- water resource management schemes; and
- pasture and livestock improvement.

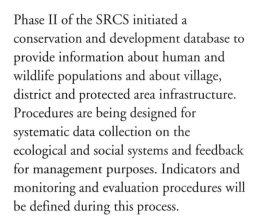

Phase II of the SRCS initiated a conservation and development database to provide information about human and wildlife populations and about village, district and protected area infrastructure. Procedures are being designed for systematic data collection on the ecological and social systems and feedback for management purposes. Indicators and monitoring and evaluation procedures will be defined during this process.

## 6 Lessons Learned

The main factors favouring the strategy were:

- the involvement of key individuals within MTNRE, IUCN, and the FZS;
- the willingness of NORAD to fund the initial workshop and follow-up activities; and
- a period of weakness in the Tanzanian economy that left the protected area infrastructure in a run-down state and led to the SRCS being seen as a means to attract outside financial resources for rehabilitation.

The main factors hindering the strategy include:

- the lack of a participatory process to agree on objectives and actions. The objectives set out do not correspond with implementation activities. This is partly due to the lack of a participatory process for deciding the objectives. It is also because much of the strategy has been designed by IUCN rather than by the communities or by the authorities who are directly concerned with managing the ecosystem. In addition, the design of the strategy has been significantly influenced by the interests of external donors. This has limited community participation in strategy implementation, and has restricted options for conserving the ecosystem resources;
- understaffing and mixing of roles, resulting in a lack of focus and some dissipation of effort. Two, and later three, full-time professional staff were expected to carry out both strategic planning and policy formulation (strategy development and implementation at a macro level) and experimental buffer zone management (protected area planning and manage-ment, wildlife use and sustainable development activities at a micro level), over a wide area and involving large numbers of different authorities and jurisdictions.

| 7 | *Chronology* |
|---|---|
| 1963 | Last record of rinderpest in Serengeti region. Wildebeest and buffalo yearling survival rate doubles. |
| 1967 | Human population west of Serengeti National Park increasing at ten per cent yearly. |
| 1976 | Tanzania–Kenya border closes. Tourist numbers decline by 65 per cent. |
| 1977 | Wildebeest population reaches 1.3 million (from 0.25 million in 1961). |
| 1980 | World Conservation Strategy (WCS) launched. |
| 1983 | Operating budget of Serengeti National Park starts to decline; by 1985 drops to low of 50 per cent of 1982 budget (US dollars). |
| 1984 | Rhino reported as nearly extinct in Serengeti National Park. Elephant populations reduced to 50 per cent of 1977 levels. |
| 1984 | Tanzania–Kenya border re-opens. |
| 1985 | Workshop on the future of the Serengeti ecosystem held at Seronera. |
| 1986 | Report of Serengeti Workshop published as '*Towards a Regional Conservation Strategy for the Serengeti*'. |
| 1989 | SRCS initiated by Ministry of Natural Resources and Tourism. Project director and technical advisor recruited. Steering committee established. |
| 1991 | SRCS phase II report and phase III action plan produced. |

# *Tanzania*

*National Conservation Strategy for
Sustainable Development and
National Environmental Action Plan*

B L M BAKOBI, NATIONAL MANAGE-
MENT ENVIRONMENT COUNCIL; TOZIRI
LWENO, NATIONAL MANAGEMENT ENVI-
RONMENT COUNCIL; AND C K TANDARI,
MINISTRY OF TOURISM, NATURAL
RESOURCES AND ENVIRONMENT

**Estimated population 1992:** 27.2
million; **Land area:** 884,000 km²;
**Ecological zones:** sandy beaches, high
grasslands, mountain ranges with volcanic
peaks, extensive Seregenti plain; **Climate:**
two rainy seasons in coastal areas, dry
season in the north, October–April;
**Annual rainfall:** 750–1500 mm; **Forest
and woodland area:** 407,500 km²; **GNP
per capita:** US$100; **Main industries:**
agriculture, reserves of iron, coal, mining,
tin and tourism; **ODA received per
capita:** US$34.90; **Population growth
rate** (1992–2000): 2.9 per cent; **Life
expectancy at birth:** 52.1 years; **Adult
literacy rate:** 64.4 per cent; **Access to safe
water:** 50 per cent; **Access to health
services:** 76 per cent; **Access to
sanitation:** 64 per cent

## Background

Tanzania has a diverse ecology with different physiographic zones and a complex topography reaching up to nearly 6,000 metres above sea level. The country has a high productive potential because of its diverse natural resources. However, with population growing at nearly three per cent per annum and changing economic conditions, there is growing pressure on the resource base, which needs to be managed carefully. As a result there is a need for the formulation of environmental strategies on a regular basis in order to define and review the environmental objectives for the country. Such strategies require a wide political basis both for legitimacy and for facilitating the continuous interministerial coordination which is necessary for cross-sectoral environmental administration.

However, Tanzania has experienced some of the most extreme problems of strategy formulation in recent years. Most important among these has been the development of a second strategy, the National Environmental Action Plan (NEAP), before the National Conservation Strategy for Sustainable Development (NCSSD) had been completed. This has led to competition and conflict within the government. In addition, both processes have involved little public consultation with the majority of the participants in the formulation processes coming from the government, parastatal and university circles. A major task now facing Tanzania is the merging of these two strategies and the establishment of clear responsibilities for the two organizations involved. Most problematic is the establishment of a cooperative working relationship between these organizations.

# NCSSD

## 1 Introduction: The NCS Process

The NCS strategy process in Tanzania has followed a linear form with the preparation of a draft strategy preceding a regional consultation stage during which specific experiences and recommendations were added. Implementation is still to be initiated some eight years after the strategy was started.

The strategy formulation process was initiated by discussions between IUCN and the Tanzanian government in 1988. This was built on growing environmental awareness and institutional development in Tanzania which saw the setting up of an interministerial committee on environmental issues in 1979, and the passing of an Act of Parliament (No 19) in 1983 leading to the establishment of the National Environment Management Council (NEMC) in 1986. Further inputs into the process have come from UNCED which has led to the renaming of the National Conservation Strategy as the National Conservation Strategy for Sustainable Development (NCSSD).

The NCSSD process is being managed by NEMC, a parastatal organization within the Ministry of Tourism, Natural Resources and Environment (MTNRE). The process has been dominated by two planning workshops as well as consultations and inputs from many experts, including the line ministries and the Planning Commission. The consultations led to the preparation of papers for the workshops by a small group of experts from within the government, parastatals and the university. Wider participation with regional and district officials was delayed until the draft NCSSD was completed and a week-long conference was held. The entire strategy formulation process involved little integration with the planning process, with no formal links established to the development planning process or to current sectoral review and planning processes in line ministries.

The Tanzanian experience in undertaking an NCSSD shows how the particular interpretations of the concepts and processes involved have given a specific character to the strategy formulation process. In addition to the emphasis upon the preparation of the strategy document, there has been a predominant view that the strategy should support existing planning mechanisms and that these will be adequate for achieving sustainable development.

## 2 Scope and Objectives of the NCSSD

Tanzania's NCSSD has seven major goals. These are to:

- involve all relevant sectors in environmental conservation;
- provide guidelines (rather than prescriptions) for sustainable socio-economic development;
- bring conservation and development into a single forum;
- establish clear roles for central government, local and regional government, NGOs, the private sector, and individuals;
- draw up NCSSD-related activities bearing in mind past, current and planned sectoral efforts undertaken to deal with environmental problems;
- harmonize demands for socio-economic development through resource use with the need for environmental conservation thereby ensuring sustainability; and
- identify enabling mechanisms through which local communities could derive benefits from their conservation efforts.

The NCSSD work focuses on six cross-sectoral, socio-political mechanisms, or strategic measures, which require central government attention in order to ensure effective environmental conservation for sustainable development. These six mechanisms are:

- planning;
- environment-related legislation and policies;
- administrative and institutional matters;
- control of resource use;
- environmental education and awareness; and
- research and technological development.

The greatest amount of attention has been focused on the first two of these, as it is believed that many of the country's environmental problems can be solved through the development of better planning.

While the foci at the national level are broad cross-sectoral mechanisms, at the regional and local government level the emphasis has been upon specific substantive issues of local concern as identified by local government, NGOs, and individuals. These issues have been analyzed in the light of the overall experience with the cross-sectoral mechanisms in order to identify appropriate problem-solving responses.

The NCSSD process in Tanzania began as an NCS process with the above goals and focal areas. It was agreed, subsequent to UNCED in 1992, that it should be extended to cover the full range of environment and development issues discussed at that meeting. Hence, in July

1992 the NCS became an NCSSD. The implications of this for the strategy process have included the extension of the range of issues to be considered and the recognition of these within a global perspective, bearing in mind the specific Tanzanian context. Some of the additions which this has led to are transboundary environmental management issues, the transportation of hazardous waste and the conservation of biodiversity.

## 3 Relationship of the NCSSD to Development Planning

The relationship of the NCSSD to the country's planning system has not yet been formalized. While the preparation of the strategy document has been undertaken in the NEMC, a variety of contacts have been established with other strategic planning initiatives undertaken in the Planning Commission in the Prime Minister's office and in various line ministries, such as the National Water Plan, and Tropical Forestry Action Plan (TFAP).

It is recognized that there is an overlap between the NCSSD and the economic planning process although the NCSSD has shown that the economic planning process pays insufficient attention to the goals of environmental sustainability and increased efficiency of resource use. There are good relations between the Planning

Commission and the NCSSD Secretariat and the two planning processes are already linked in the NCSSD Steering Committee which includes representatives of all relevant ministries. Discussions have now begun about the contribution which the NCSSD should make to the new three-year rolling planning process. The long term intention is to integrate the NCSSD into this new planning process.

## 4 Initial Development

### Start up

In 1979, subsequent to the first UNCED at Stockholm in 1972, Tanzania established an interministerial committee for environmental issues. The committee was based in the Ministry of Lands, Housing and Local Government. This institutional initiative grew with the formation of a ministry responsible for the environment which continues to be responsible for the interministerial committee on the environment. This ministry has since been given responsibility for tourism and natural resources so that environment is now only one department within the ministry.

In 1983 the Act establishing an NEMC was passed; in November 1986 this Council was inaugurated within the Ministry of Lands, Housing and Local Government. Subsequently, NEMC was subsumed into MTNRE, where it remains today as a parastatal organization with an advisory responsibility to the government. This parastatal position means that NEMC falls outside the narrow sectoral confines of the ministry so that it can take a more multi-disciplinary approach, recognizing, as it does, the link of environment to socio-economic development.

The establishment of the NEMC came in response to a growing awareness in government that the various mechanisms for environmental management, such as planning, legislation and administration, were being handled unisectorally, with little or no coordination or cooperation between sectors. It was recognized that this led to inefficient and irrational use of resources, unsustainable development and environmental problems. As a result when NEMC was established it was charged with coordinating and harmonizing competing sectoral activities.

One of the first goals of NEMC was to develop an environmental profile of Tanzania which was undertaken in 1988 with DANIDA support. Following this there was a major debate about how to bring the various actors concerned with the environment into a dialogue which would lead to cooperation over critical environmental issues. The need for some form of consultation process became clear as did the need for an agreed document which would specify the principles which should guide the activities and policies of government agencies. In the end it was decided by NEMC, following discussions with IUCN, that an NCS would be the best way to develop this process, and IUCN was approached to assist in the search for funding. This was obtained from SIDA in 1988, and an Exploratory Planning Mission for the NCS formulation process was undertaken in late 1989.

### Structure of the NCSSD

The NCSSD process has been established as a project within NEMC. The day-to-day operations of the NCSSD are managed by a Secretariat which is chaired by the Director General of NEMC and based in that institution. The National Coordinator of the NCSSD is the Director for Natural Resources in NEMC, who is also the Secretary for the Secretariat. In addition the NCSSD Secretariat has two other full-time staff both drawn from NEMC, while the other 11 members of NEMC are part-time members of the Secretariat. The project has been supported by one expatriate technical advisor since late 1990 and a second expatriate advisor joined in September 1992.

The project is directed by a steering committee. This is chaired by the Principal Secretary of MTNRE, while the Secretary to the Committee is the

Director General of NEMC. There are nearly 30 members of the steering committee, including principal secretaries and directors from relevant government ministries and departments as well as senior academics.

There is also a technical committee composed of over 30 professionals from relevant organizations including government departments, parastatal organizations, NGOs and the university. In no case do any of the NCSSD committees include representatives from the business sector or community-based organizations.

During the NCSSD process to date, the steering committee has met four times and the technical committee three times. Recently these two committees appear to have merged and the distinction between their two functions has become blurred.

*The NCSSD Process*

The NCSSD process began in June 1989 with an exploratory and planning mission by IUCN. This led to the identification of the methodology, approach and philosophy appropriate for the NCS as it was then.

In the early phases of its work the NCSSD process had to be very careful to avoid departmental sensitivities. As a result it concentrated its attention upon cross-sectoral areas, especially broad strategic issues such as institutional structures and planning frameworks. The NCSSD has stressed the facilitating role it has to play in supporting actions by individual government agencies, noting that it neither seeks to reinvent the wheel, nor to usurp the power of line ministries, but rather encourage and support all actions which are in line with the principles of the NCSSD.

The NCSSD process in Tanzania has involved two major workshops in 1990 and 1992 which have been supported by periods of study to develop background papers. In November 1990 the first workshop was convened in Dodoma with the aim of launching the NCS process, reviewing current issues in environmental management and determining the future steps to be taken. This meeting involved between 40 and 50 representatives from different government departments, some parastatals and the university. The papers which they presented at this meeting were mainly concerned with the negative impacts of human use upon the natural resource base, with particular emphasis upon pollution and resource degradation.

In addition, this meeting made recommendations about the issues which should be addressed in the NCS and the structure of the NCS document. The meeting also identified six cross-sectoral mechanisms as the means by which the goals of the NCS might be achieved (these are outlined above). The general emphasis in this meeting was on the importance of structural issues, such as planning processes, legislation, institutions and administration for addressing the problems, rather than on substantive responses such as pollution control and wildlife conservation.

The workshop also recognized that the NCS process should be more than the preparation of a document and should involve a long-term ongoing process which requires interaction between the Secretariat and technical committee and the rest of government and society as a whole. However, despite this recognition of the need for participation and the initiating role of this meeting, its proceedings have still not yet been published and there has been little wide-ranging participation of the public in the NCSSD process. The only exception to this is the regional conference discussed below.

Following this first workshop it was proposed that consultation should be undertaken in order to develop further research and background reports for a second workshop. There were 23 topics identified for further work, mainly covering the various ways in which environmental planning and protection can be achieved. For each topic the researchers were required to outline the issues, identify strategy packages and action plans and identify possible constraints.

The original schedule for this work was truncated by a request from government that the draft NCS document should be completed by June 1992. Hence consultation was limited to senior professionals; the technical committee workshop, to review the background papers, was brought forward, being held at Tanga in April 1992. The focus of this meeting was on the solutions to the environmental problems discussed at the first workshop. Subsequently, three short-term consultants were hired to consolidate the material into the various volumes of the NCS envisaged at that stage, including a preliminary draft NCS.

Following the preparation of the preliminary draft, a meeting of the steering committee was convened to scrutinize the document and outline the steps to finalize it. This meeting, held in July 1992, led to the suggestion that the NCS should be broadened to cover the full range of sustainability issues raised at UNCED and so become an NCSSD. This was formally agreed in December 1992. Subsequently, the NCSSD has benefited from the Tanzanian UNCED follow-up conference and documentation, organized by the newly-created Division of Environment in MTNRE, this being the ministry to which NEMC is answerable.

Besides the work on the NCS document, the Secretariat has also given briefings to the Cabinet and Parliament so that these senior political bodies, as well as the President and Prime Minister are sensitized to the idea of an NCSSD. Such briefings and the political support they have generated have been important in improving the response from organizations and officials approached in the process, as originally cooperation was often difficult to obtain because of the absence of initial sensitization activities at the start of the NCS process.

Despite the recognition at various times that the NCSSD process needs to be more participatory and involve activities which raise awareness and develop the capacity of people to address the ideas therein, the focus of activity has remained the production of the strategy document.

The draft NCSSD was widely scrutinized by a series of bodies including the NCSSD Technical and Steering Committees, the NEMC Council, donors and invited eminent persons. It was reviewed by the Board of Directors of NEMC and approved on 30 September 1993. In mid-November a series of meetings were held with representatives of sectoral ministries who gave their comments on the draft, especially the recommendations for action which affected their respective ministries directly. Written additions to the draft were also commissioned from the sectoral ministries. A revised draft was then approved at a steering committee meeting in February 1994.

This draft of the NCSSD was then presented to representatives of district and regional governments at a week-long conference at Arusha at the end of February. The aim of the meeting was to understand the feelings of people at the grassroots level and to listen to their advice. In recognition of the fact that local government is not only closer to the people, but also the custodian of the natural resources, the conference drew most of its participants from the district authorities. Most districts and all regions were represented at the conference, the majority of the participants being district executive officers, town directors, and district planning officers. In addition the conference had representatives from the President's Office, a few sectoral ministries, NGOs, and donor observers. The conference involved small-group discussions concerning the most pressing environmental problems facing the district representatives and the relationship of these problems to the ideas presented in the draft NCSSD.

The fourth and final meeting of the NCSSD Steering Committee took place on 2 May 1995. This approved the changes incorporated in the light of the Arusha conference and made some minor adjustments so that the final draft could be submitted to the government in June. It consists of a single volume with five chapters, the last one being an Action Plan.

## 5  Implementation and Results of the NCSSD

Specific methods for implementation of the NCSSD have yet to be defined. However, with the support of NEMC, ways of applying the ideas found in the NCSSD are beginning to be taken up by the regions and the districts. In addition, there is recognition that the NCSSD should contribute towards the new three-year rolling planning process which has been introduced in Tanzania, and methods by which this can be achieved are being sought. Although no formal links exist yet between the NCSSD Secretariat and the Planning Commission in the Prime Minister's office, informal links exist in the NCSSD Steering Committee which includes representatives of all relevant ministries, including the Planning Commission. Links between the NCSSD, the Prime Minister's office and the Planning Commission are essential for the successful implementation of the NCSSD as this will require some authority to be exerted over the line ministries and other government agencies to ensure that their activities apply the principles outlined in the NCSSD.

## 6  Lessons Learned

The experience with the Tanzania NCSSD clearly shows the dangers of seeing the NCSSD as a document and of not giving adequate attention to the process. By focusing upon document preparation and by using a narrow range of expertise from government, parastatals and the university, the NEMC has failed to develop the widespread awareness in the society which is needed to mobilize support for the NCSSD process. On the other hand, the regional and district conference has stimulated interest at the sub-national level; initiatives already exist to develop conservation strategies in the coastal region, Kiteto and Simanjiro districts, and some districts in Tabora Region.

The participatory aspect of the NCSSD has been quite variable. At the national level, the process did try to bring every type of stakeholder into the discussions, although this was primarily through two specific workshops and was not supported by frequent meetings of the Steering and technical committees. The conference of regional and district officials held at Arusha in early 1995, helped identify locally pressing problems, but their often vigorous presentation was a very belated and restricted attempt to provide any grassroots input into this process, and lacked a downward reach to the community level. It is clear that an earlier start to participation, and wider involvement in that participation, should have been allowed by the government in the NCSSD process rather than restricting it to regional and district level representatives after NEMC had produced the draft document.

Another lesson from the Tanzanian experience is the way in which the NCSSD process initially focused on existing planning mechanisms. These were seen as the major way for the state to support the achievement of sustainable development. A much broader range of activities, especially with respect to public awareness, capacity development, local participation and policy measures, should have been considered from the start and their use and potential contribution within the ongoing NCSSD process discussed.

While the NCSSD process has benefitted from the experience of other broad planning activities within Tanzania in recent years, such as the TFAP, Water Master Plan and Plan of Action to Combat Desertification, it has failed to formally link with them. There has been no attempt to develop a broad coordinating framework role for the NCSSD within which these initiatives could be situated for maximum coordination and impact. This situation may be altered in the near future, as there are attempts underway to create contact units in all sectoral ministries.

Finally, but most importantly, the Tanzanian experience with the NCSSD shows that having an apparently favourable institutional setting with NEMC and MTNRE, and growing political support in the early years of the process, has not been sufficient to ensure rapid progress and success of the NCSSD. In the end, further institutional development, namely the creation of a new Division of Environment within MTNRE, with its control over policy related issues and its involvement in the NEAP process (see below), has led to competition and conflict. As a result, it is clear that decisions about strategy development need to be clearly publicised and also enforced with high level political backing which is not diverted as a result of donor pressure.

## NEAP

### 1 Introduction to the NEAP Process

The NEAP in Tanzania provides the framework required for making the fundamental changes needed to bring environmental considerations into mainstream decision-making. While the main focus of the NCSSD has been to identify the problems which have to be considered and outline broad approaches, or strategies, to address these, the aim of the NEAP is to identify specific actions which need to be undertaken by different organizations, in both the short and the long term.

The NEAP has been based on the following:

- the numerous project and policy responses to environmental concerns;
- the National Conservation Strategy consultation process and its working documents; and
- the Agenda 21 National Plan consultation process and outputs.

These have all been integrated into the NEAP, with the NCSSD in particular providing a large proportion of the scientific material required.

## 2 Development Phase

### Origins of the Strategy

The NEAP was begun in February 1993 and from the outset had a submission date of June 1995. As with other NEAPs the major concern which led to its initiation was the wish of the Tanzanian government to remain eligible for IDA funds from the World Bank.

The aim of the NEAP has been to produce a comprehensive document which looks at environment and development from a national perspective, and identifies the ways in which the broad strategies for addressing environmental issues can be articulated in specific actions, with their implementational requirements and also regular monitoring and review. In particular, the NEAP sets out to address the growing concerns in the country for mitigating environmental degradation.

The process which the NEAP has promoted provides for the determination of environmental priorities for action in every sector, evaluating costs and benefits, the trade-offs between often conflicting concerns affecting society, undertaking sectoral and cross-sectoral plans and policy analysis, and preventing or reducing conflicts.

The tasks which the NEAP has, or will, involve in order to achieve its objectives include: participation, information assembly, analysis and sharing, policy formulation, action planning and budgeting, monitoring and evaluation, the formulation of legislation and capacity-building. In the final analysis the aim is to move environment and development from a point of conflict to one of mutual support.

### Sponsorship and Location

The NEAP was initiated in the Division of Environment in the Ministry of Tourism, Natural Resources and

Environment, with sponsorship from the World Bank. This location was chosen following the failure of discussions in early 1993 with NEMC which had rejected the need for an NEAP given the advanced state of the NCSSD.

### Process of Strategy Formulation

The NEAP process of strategy formulation has aimed at addressing seven environmental problems, namely: soil erosion, desertification, deforestation, water pollution (both marine and freshwater), air pollution, urban pollution, and loss of biodiversity.

The NEAP process was carried out at the national level in a cross-sectoral manner. The staff involved in the process were drawn from the Division of Environment and the NEMC, both in the Ministry of Tourism, Natural Resources and Environment, the Ministries of Agriculture, Lands, Water, Energy and Minerals, Trade and Industries, and some NGOs.

The analytical method used was qualitative in order to identify the major environmental problems of concern to the nation. Participatory methods were used at the sectoral and cross-sectoral levels with staff from the various sectors involved in preparing the NEAP document. Because of the timescale and the approach followed, with a team of

experts supported by World Bank advisors, participation was limited, with no involvement at the grassroots levels, including villagers and district officials. In addition, the degree of cross-sectoral involvement was restricted.

### Training and Demonstration Activities

The development phase of the NEAP has provided capacity-building to the staff who were involved in this exercise. These experts come from various professions and sectors in the economy.

### Strengths of the Development Phase

The major strengths associated with this phase were:

- strong awareness about environmental issues prior to the preparation process;
- broad participation in the process at national and regional levels;
- increased awareness of environmental issues;
- the process promoted an integrated approach for donor support; and
- the process further developed a dialogue between different stakeholders about sustainable development.

In many cases these strengths built upon sensitivities and awareness stimulated by the NCSSD and Agenda 21 Plan processes.

*Weaknesses of the Development Phase*

The major weaknesses associated with this phase were:

- the way in which the NEAP process was initiated by the World Bank;
- the duplication of the NEAP and NCSSD initiatives by the Division of the Environment and NEMC respectively;
- limited awareness of sustainable development issues among the general public;
- inadequate public participation;
- inadequate social and economic analysis; and
- limited information flow during the preparation phase.

## 3 Lessons Learned

Six major lessons were learned in the NEAP preparation process. These are that:

- increased attention should be given during the development phase to capacity-building for the staff involved, especially in the area of environmental management;
- strong support at the political level is crucial for the success of environmental and sustainable development initiatives;
- broad participation of people at various levels of the preparation is essential;

- the new approach of cross-sectoral thinking and techniques is increasingly recognized as valuable;
- balancing environmental, economic and social concerns is a major challenge; and
- there is a need to harmonize efforts both by government agencies and donor communities.

## 4 Implementation Phase

A number of tasks can be identified as necessary for the implementation of the NEAP. These include:

- education and publicity to increase environmental awareness;
- appointment of an environment officer in every institution;
- production by the Ministry of Tourism, Natural Resources and Environment of an annual report on the NEAP's progress;
- annual reports by each ministry on environmental issues; and
- prioritizing of environmental concerns by the administrations in all districts and regions.

The new institutional arrangements which are supposed to be in place include:

- environmental impact assessment (EIA);

- environmental protection legislation;
- economic instruments for environmental analysis; and
- indicators and standards for environmental monitoring; and
- public participation and awareness.

The use of EIA is seen as the main way in which the strategy will be integrated into mainstream economic development with every proposed investment project having to produce an acceptable assessment. In terms of legislation an inventory of environmental laws and ordinances has been prepared. This will be used as the basis for designing framework legislation for environmental protection.

Other important initiatives which are needed for successful implementation include capacity-building and harmonization of initiatives. Capacity-building is needed in the areas of coordination, enforcement, economic analysis, management of resources, cleaner production, and general environmental management. Arrangements are now being made by the government and donor agencies to support the training of NEAP staff and other implementors.

Harmonization of the several initiatives or projects concerned with sustainable development, biodiversity, desertification issues remains to be achieved. In most cases there are no conflicts as each of these is properly funded and staff have been allocated to them. They are integrated via the Division of Environment and NEMC. There are no implementational problems since each organization has a clearly defined mandate and the staff are assigned tasks according to their terms of reference. The major outstanding issue is the relationship between the NCSSD and the NEAP.

## 5 Strengths and Weaknesses of Implementation

Since the NEAP has not yet reached the implementational stage, it is hard to tell the strengths and weaknesses at this stage. It is hoped that one of the major strengths will be an improved coordination and linkage across sectors in the economy, all aimed at sustainable use of natural resources and environmental sustainability. The major weakness seems to be that the programme looks over-ambitious and very demanding in terms of cross-sectoral linkages.

## 6 Conclusions

While the NEAP has several objectives, it tries to achieve coordination which will ensure that development in any one sector does not occur at the expense of development in another sector, and that development now is not bought at the expense of future generations. The NEAP seeks to improve the interlinkages between environment and development. It encompasses a broad spectrum of concerns, engages everyone concerned, and seeks to build capacities to handle the complex issues of sustainable development in Tanzania.

In the final analysis, the NEAP will achieve its objectives if it can move environment and development from a point of conflict to one of mutual support. It implies, therefore, that economic development has to occur together with sustainable use of natural resources and environmental sustainability.

## General Conclusions

Tanzania is a classic example of two strategic processes having been started at different times with different schedules, although similar long-term aims. The failure to integrate the NEAP into the NCSSD process has led to competition and conflict between the people and institutions involved in the two processes.

What is needed now is an integration and harmonization process which provides a clear division of labour and responsibility between the two institutions involved to ensure that duplication of effort does not occur. Some progress towards this appears to be emerging with the policy and national focus in the NEAP and a regional and district-level focus for the NCSSD, including local-level implementation.

| 7 | *Chronology* |
|---|---|
| 1979 | Interministerial committee for environmental issues established. |
| 1983 | Act No 19 establishing National Environment Management Council (NEMC) passed through Parliament. |
| 1986 | NEMC established. |
| 1988 | Environmental profile prepared by NEMC with DANIDA support. Discussions with IUCN over National Conservation Strategy (NCS). |
| 1989 | NCS process begun with IUCN mission. |
| 1990 | Dodoma Workshop. |
| 1991 | Ministry of Tourism, Natural Resources and Environment (MTNRE) established. |
| 1992 | Tanga Workshop. Preparation of preliminary draft. Decision to make NCS process an NCSSD process. |
| 1993 | Initiation of the NEAP within Division of Environment in MTNRE. First draft NCSSD produced. |
| 1994 | Regional and District Workshop on NCSSD held at Arusha. |
| 1995 | NCSSD submitted to government for approval process. NEAP approved by Cabinet. |

# Uganda

*National Environmental Action Plan*

DAVID OGARAM, MINISTRY OF NATURAL RESOURCES; AND ROBERT WABUNOHA, MINISTRY OF NATURAL RESOURCES

**Estimated population 1992:** 19.3 million; **Land area:** 200,000 km²; **Ecological zones:** land-locked, mainly plateau with volcanic ridges, dry savannah, semi-desert in north, fertile Lake Victoria basin in southeast; **Climate:** warm, with temperatures moderated by high elevation and lakes; **Annual rainfall:** 1000–1500 mm; **Forest and woodland area:** 55,000 km²; **GNP per capita:** US$180; **Main industries:** agriculture, tungsten, copper, tin; **ODA received per capita:** US$35.50; **Population growth rate** (1992–2000): 3.1 per cent; **Life expectancy at birth:** 44.9 years; **Adult literacy rate:** 58.6 per cent; **Access to safe water:** 31 per cent; **Access to health services:** 49 per cent; **Access to sanitation:** 57 per cent

## 1 Introduction

Uganda's efforts to develop a strategy for sustainability have involved several initiatives during the last decade. These have included the IUCN- and UNEP-supported National Conservation Strategy in 1984/85, UNEP's work on Environmental Profiles in the late 1980s, and the current National Environmental Action Plan initiated by the World Bank.

The NEAP process was started in mid-1991 as the World Bank became increasingly involved in Uganda's structural adjustment. The government responded positively to the Bank's proposal for an NEAP, since it saw this as coinciding with its own goals for rehabilitating the country's natural resources.

The NEAP process was initially based in the Ministry of Water, Energy, Minerals and Environment Protection, where an NEAP Secretariat was created in 1991 with nine sectoral task forces. The task forces prepared background and issue papers through extensive fieldwork. These papers were discussed at regional workshops and a national conference, and the outcome of these deliberations was consolidated into a draft NEAP document. This consisted of a Policy Document, a National Environment Bill, an institutional framework and an Investment Plan. This draft went through a new series of consultations and the NEAP was finally sent to Cabinet and approved in mid-1994.

Since 1992, and simultaneously with the above process, a series of key policy and legislation documents have been issued. The most important, approved by Parliament in May 1995, is the Environmental Management Statute, which regulates all environmental aspects in the country. The statute provides an institutional framework for implementing the NEAP by establishing the National Environmental Management Authority (NEMA) as the institution responsible for coordination, monitoring and supervision of all activities related to environmental management.

Several sets of guidelines to provide orientation to different processes have also been produced. Among these are the Guidelines for Decentralization of Environmental Management, aimed primarily at the district levels; the Guidelines for Environmental Impact Assessment to be used by the line ministries, and the Guidelines for Development of By-Laws, ie local regulations that do not require Parliamentary approval.

Along with these initiatives, a State of the Environment Report was produced in 1994, and this will be updated every five years. The preparation of District Environmental Action Plans (DEAPs) has also been commenced in two districts, with the conception phase started in the other 37 districts. These DEAPs started with the preparation of District Environmental Profiles (eight completed up to September 1995), which gathered all available district information about the environment as a basis for the DEAPs. District Environmental Information Centres were created in every district for this purpose.

A review of the existing laws related to the environment has also been launched aiming to make them compatible with the new statute.

A key aspect of the process is the incorporation of several activities of the NEAP in the Public Investment Plan for 1995, meaning that some environment-related activities now being implemented are funded by the governmental national budget.

The NEAP process has been very open: the Ugandan authorities have welcomed specialist inputs from a variety of organizations. In addition to World Bank leadership and USAID funding and technical support, the NEAP has involved a number of international agencies with specialist skills, such as IUCN.

The experience of Uganda in developing an NEAP, shortly after a period of major political change, provides a number of lessons. These include the importance of a strongly felt need in both society and the government to improve the environmental situation in the country. This has translated into political support for the NEAP process at all levels of government. The Resistance Committees, which exist at all levels in Ugandan society, have facilitated the participation of communities. The government policy of decentralization encouraged the holding of regional workshops to discuss the papers prepared by the task forces. The whole process has run smoothly and key legislation has been approved.

There was some concern in 1992 that the NEAP could not be seen as a long term and evolving strategy but simply as a document with a number of project activities to be implemented over five years. The subsequent advances in the integration of environmental issues and concerns into the legal framework and the governmental structure of the country show a different process. The most recent progress in this direction has been the establishment of NEMA in December 1995 which has taken over the functions of the now disbanded NEAP Secretariat and many other duties concerned with coordinating, initiating and advocating environmental activities.

## 2 Scope and Objectives

The overall objective of the NEAP is to integrate environmental sustainability into socio-economic planning. This will be guided by a strategy that reconciles economic development with the conservation of biological diversity and the sustainable use of natural resources.

Specific objectives for the NEAP include:

- enhancing the health and quality of life of the Ugandan people;
- preserving and restoring the equilibrium of ecosystems, and maintaining ecological processes and life support systems;
- integrating environmental concerns in all development-oriented policies and plans at national and local levels; and
- reducing waste and achieving a sustainable level of resource consumption.

These objectives make it clear that the NEAP process aims to be comprehensive, integrated and multi-sectoral in nature. It seeks to address environmental issues in a variety of ways, paying attention to policy, legislation and institutional reforms, as well as the development and implementation of investment programmes. The NEAP, through its implementing structures, such as NEMA, also includes the assessment of current and future development projects and programmes. These will be reviewed to ensure that they pay appropriate attention to environmental considerations. All these features ensure the continuity and evolution of the NEAP as a permanent process to deal with Uganda's environmental issues.

A key objective of the NEAP is to develop improved participation and coordination when addressing environmental issues. The NEAP process recognizes that sustainable development will be achieved only if people participate in the management of the country's natural resources, and if an integrative, multi-sectoral approach is taken. The current approach to natural resource management is often top-down and sectoral, with *ad hoc* responses to problems, a lack of coordination between sectors in the government administration and little community participation. Hence a fundamental change in approach is sought through the action of the recently created structures, especially NEMA.

## 3 Relationship to Development Planning

The Ministry of Finance, Planning and Economic Development is responsible for formulating economic and social development plans, as well as monitoring implementation. A section of this ministry is responsible for natural resources, but not environmental planning or management. Responsibility is not centralized and several ministries play a role, a situation which the NEAP has had to address.

Although the NEAP seeks to improve the coordination of environmental issues in development planning, it was envisaged that no sectoral ministry should have sole responsibility for the environment. This approach was institutionalized with the establishment of NEMA as the coordinating, monitoring and supervising (but not implementing) institution. In addition to these tasks, it will undertake reviews of policies, legal frameworks and institutional arrangements. The purpose of these reviews will be to ensure that the policies, laws and institutions are sensitive and holistic, and take account of the interests of other sectors.

## 4 Initial Development

### Start-Up

Uganda had been involved in discussions with IUCN about the development of some form of environmental strategy since 1980 when former President Obote took part in launching the World Conservation Strategy. In 1983, IUCN undertook an NCS design mission. With UNEP funding, IUCN provided an NCS advisor

in 1984 who helped the government start an NCS process until unrest in 1985 forced him to leave.

Since the National Resistance Movement (NRM) came to power in 1986, Uganda has undergone a period of reconstruction. Serious and accelerating degradation threatens the livelihoods of many people. Consequently, the new government recognized from the start that increased attention had to be given to environmental issues. The causes of this degradation are complex, involving the interaction of poverty, ignorance, poor management, unfavourable government policies and lack of appropriate institutions. Hence a broad approach was seen as essential for improving the environmental situation in the country.

One response has been institutional development. In 1986, a Ministry of Environment Protection (MEP) was established to coordinate environmental concerns and develop policy and legal frameworks. In 1989, that ministry was restructured and became a department in the Ministry of Water, Energy, Minerals and Environmental Protection. The Secretary in charge of environmental issues has equal rank to the Ministry's Permanent Secretary.

The NRM Government contacted IUCN soon after coming to power and sought support in wetland management training and forest management pilot projects. This led to the development of a Strategy for the Management and Conservation of Wetlands, and the Uganda Forest Conservation Programme. The government made it clear that the NCS was not on its agenda; and the original NCS project was formally terminated in September 1986.

MEP pursued a national approach to environmental issues through links with UNEP which it asked to prepare a series of environmental profiles. These were to provide a baseline for any further government consideration of a national environmental strategy. By the time these profiles were produced in 1990, the World Bank had become involved in a structural adjustment process, and had started discussions on the formulation of an NEAP as part of this process. These discussions, along with the government's increasing concern for rehabilitating the country's natural resources, led in mid-1991 to the beginning of work on the NEAP, which was approved in mid-1994.

*Organization*

The NEAP process was administered by the Department of Environment in the Ministry of Water, Energy, Minerals and Environment Protection (WEMEP). The overall direction of NEAP activities was guided by a policy-level steering committee. This was a Cabinet subcommittee chaired by the Prime Minister with the Minister of WEMEP as the Secretary. The committee included all the ministers with environmental responsibilities: Finance and Planning; Agriculture; Animal Industry and Fisheries; Education and Sports; Land, Housing and Urban Development; Tourism, Wildlife and Antiquities; Justice and Constitutional Affairs; Women in Development, Youth and Culture; Commerce, Industry and Cooperatives; Works and Transport; and Local Government and Information.

The production of the NEAP document was based on the work of nine sectoral task forces. They were responsible for:

- environmental policy, legislation and institutional arrangements;
- environmental education, research and human resource development;
- land management, agriculture, livestock and rangelands;
- aquatic biodiversity, wetlands, water and water resources;
- terrestrial biodiversity, forestry, wildlife and tourism;
- mining, industry, hazardous materials and toxic chemicals;
- population, health and human settlement;
- energy and climatic change; and
- environmental information.

The task forces were established by November 1991. At that time they each had nine members drawn from government, NGOs, the private sector, and academia, all members being senior officials and experts. The task forces were responsible for preparing two types of documents: background and topic papers, which are analytical documents reviewing the broad areas of responsibility of each task force; and issue papers, which address specific problems and make recommendations for action.

After they had drafted these documents, the task forces were each reduced to two or four persons, chosen for the relevance of their specialist knowledge to the remaining work in regional workshops and drafting of the NEAP. These remaining members of the task forces formed the NEAP Secretariat: 12 were government officials, 12 were from academia, and two were from the private sector, including NGOs. In addition, the Secretariat included local resource persons and, since October 1992, three technical advisors provided by USAID. The Secretariat was under the direction of the Secretary for Environmental Protection. Day-to-day management was undertaken by a coordinator from the Department of the Environment in WEMEP.

In addition, monitoring and evaluation structures were established with an Advisory Committee. This consisted of 30 people drawn from all sectors of the community except the government, with

representatives of donor agencies, NGOs, academic institutions and the private sector.

*The NEAP process*

Formulating the NEAP involved:

- defining the principal environmental issues and problems, and preparing topic and issue papers which analyze causes and make recommendations;
- compilation of the first draft of an NEAP document by the Secretariat from the work of the task forces;
- reviewing draft recommendations through local, regional and national seminars leading to a revised draft;
- reviewing the draft NEAP document at an international conference;
- final review and revisions, and presentation to the government for approval; and
- government approval and action on policies, legislation, and institutions.

The first stage of preparing draft topic and issue papers involved the task forces in literature reviews and field research in each of the country's 38 districts. The collection of field information and holding workshops to obtain the views of key individuals was facilitated by the network of Resistance Committees which were set up under the NRM government. These exist at all levels down to the village and so provide important fora for discussing issues concerning the NEAP.

Assistance in this stage of the NEAP process was provided by two short term specialists from the World Resources Institute and later by a joint WRI/IUCN team. They provided detailed advice on policy and legislation as well as more general guidance concerning institutional arrangements and economics.

The task force papers were presented at nine regional workshops between July and September 1992 to obtain comments and feedback in the light of local experience. Workshop participants were drawn from 36 of the 38 districts. They included local leaders, government departmental officials from the district and regional levels, NGO representatives, resource users, and women's representatives. Each regional workshop lasted three days and involved at least 100 participants. The meetings were chaired by local officials to ensure that their direction reflected local needs and perceptions. In addition to the regional workshops there were two one-day presentations by the NEAP Task Forces and Secretariat to Commissioners (Heads of Departments in ministries) and also to Members of Parliament and the President.

Once feedback from the regional workshop phase had been incorporated in revised papers, a National Conference was held in November 1992. This was opened by the President and attended by 400 representatives of donor agencies, NGOs, the business sector, youth, women's groups, resource users, academics, and government staff at ministry and district levels.

The NEAP document and an Investment Programme were drafted in the light of the regional workshops and National Conference. Both documents were ready by June 1993. The NEAP document was sent to Cabinet and approved one year later in 1994.

After Cabinet approval of the NEAP, the Investment Plan was considered by the Ministry of Finance which appointed a specialist in budget planning to work with the NEAP team. As a result of this joint work, several aspects of the NEAP Investment Plan were incorporated in the 1995 Investment Plan of the Ministry of Finance to be funded from the national budget. The implementation of these activities started in 1995 with the Ugandan fiscal year.

## 5 Implementation

The NEAP will be implemented by the relevant ministries, NGOs, the business sector and the local communities.

Coordinating mechanisms will be required to ensure these organizations and groups apply the principles of the NEAP and that initiatives are mutually supportive rather than conflicting. The body responsible for this is NEMA, established in December 1995.

In addition the institutional development is expected to involve the establishment of environmental officers who will sit on the district development committees and on environment committees at district and lower levels. Environment liaison officers will also be established within ministries at the national level to implement the NEAP. In addition, the Ministry of Women in Development, Youth and Culture will ensure that gender issues are integrated into all aspects of the NEAP recommendations.

*Institutional setting*

NEMA is responsible not only for the coordination of the efforts of all ministries to implement the NEAP, but also for the supervision and monitoring of the implementing activities. It has a Policy Committee on Environment which includes ten of the twenty national Ministers, including Finance and all the sectoral ministries with significant environmental concerns. This Committee is responsible for developing and approving NEMA policies.

Reporting to the Policy Committee is a Board of Directors, composed of nine members (three from governmental ministries, two from national universities, two from NGOs and two from the private sector). This Board supervizes the activities of NEMA. Within NEMA there is an Executive Director and four divisions: legal; information and monitoring (including monitoring and evaluation); education, training, awareness and mass mobilization; and finance and administration. The Board can organize technical committees on an *ad hoc* basis to address specific issues which are beyond NEMA's capacity.

*Process integration and harmonization*

All of the environmental activities of the government are now under the umbrella of the Environmental Management Bill that was developed subsequent to the preparation of the NEAP. This statute, which was endorsed by Parliament and enacted by the President in May 1995, provides for the sustainable management of the environment and the establishment of an authority as the principal agency in Uganda for the management of the environment. This authority, NEMA, is charged with coordinating, monitoring and supervising all activities in the field of environment. A typical example of the responsibilities which have been passed over to NEMA is the ongoing Wetlands Strategy, started several years ago.

*Financing Implementation of the NEAP*

While some activities of the NEAP Investment Plan were incorporated in the National Investment Plan, Uganda will still rely heavily on external cooperation if the NEAP is going to advance significantly in the next years. The government is providing counterpart funding in addition to the usual office accommodation and similar in some projects (ie Uganda is contributing 15 per cent of the budget required for the capacity-building project planned to start in late 1995). While this contribution is significant in relation to the country's budget, it is not sufficient to ensure the sustainability of NEAP implementation at an acceptable rate.

*Capacity Development*

A comprehensive capacity-building project is due to be launched late in 1995 with World Bank support, and with the EIA component funded by UNDP. This project aims to develop capacities for environmental planning, implementation and monitoring at both national and districts levels.

*Communications*

There has been a systematic communications effort since 1993. A weekly page on the environment is published every Friday in one of the main country newspapers. There is a quarterly Environmental

Newsletter, funded by USAID, distributed throughout the country to schools, districts, ministries, etc. Radio and television are used to provide broader coverage for some specific events. This can only be on an *ad hoc* basis, however, due to the costs involved.

*Monitoring and Evaluation*

The NEAP progress is monitored through several mechanisms built into the Plan. The most comprehensive one is the State of the Environment Report, the first of which was produced in 1994. This will be updated every five years.

The NEAP will be reviewed every two-and-a-half years, with the first review scheduled for 1997. NEMA has an Annual Action Plan for the implementation of NEAP activities, the schedule of which is monitored by the NEMA Board of Directors. The DEAPs will be reviewed every two years.

*6 Lessons Learned*

The NEAP process has made rapid progress (the necessary material for drafting the action plan was assembled and reviewed within a year of establishing the task forces). This speed is due to widespread commitment to the NEAP, within the government, including the President and Cabinet, and in the communities.

Progress has also been facilitated by the Resistance Committees at different levels and by the decentralization policy of the government. Both these influences have encouraged active participation in regional meetings by local representatives.

The critical review of government structure, ongoing in Uganda since 1986, has also stimulated the NEAP process by generating widespread concern about the neglect of environmental issues in planning and policy development. The NEAP process itself has shown the importance of working comprehensively, and allocating the necessary time to make an exhaustive analysis of the situation.

The Ugandan government has involved a range of organizations in the NEAP, including the WRI and IUCN, as well the World Bank, USAID and UNEP. This willingness to learn from all sources about

ideas of environmental management that may be relevant for Uganda is found among both government officials and resource users.

The institutional framework needs further thought, negotiation, and consensus-building as NEMA becomes operational. While it is important not to lose momentum, it is necessary to avoid being pressured into arrangements which will hamper implementation later.

Finally, there should not be a rush to produce the investment programme. This, also, must be thought and negotiated carefully. A key aspect here is the involvement of the Ministry of Finance in this process as early as possible. This involvement will facilitate the subsequent incorporation of investment plan activities into the national budget and implementation system.

| 7 | *Chronology* |
|---|---|
| 1980 | President Obote participates in launching the World Conservation Strategy. |
| 1983 | IUCN NCS design mission. |
| 1984 | IUCN provides NCS advisor with UNEP funding. |
| 1985 | NCS advisor withdrawn for security reasons. |
| 1986 | National Resistance Movement government comes to power. |
|  | Establishment of Ministry of Environment Protection (MEP). NCS process formally closed. IUCN provides support for wetland management training and forestry management pilot projects. |
| 1989 | MEP becomes part of Ministry of Water, Energy, Minerals and Environment Protection (WEMEP). |
| 1990 | UNEP produces environmental profiles. World Bank begins discussions on NEAP with Government of Uganda. |
| 1991 | NEAP process begins. Nine task forces established and Secretariat set up in WEMEP. |
| 1992 | Regional Workshops and National Conference held to discuss work of task forces. |
| 1993 | NEAP Document and Investment Plan presented to Cabinet. |
| 1994 | Cabinet approves NEAP Document. Ministry of Finance incorporates parts of the Investment Plan in the Public Investment Plan for 1995. |
| 1995 | Environmental Management Statute approved by Parliament. National Environmental Management Authority (NEMA) created to coordinate, supervize and monitor all activities related with environmental management. |
|  | Preparation of District Environmental Action Plans begun. |

# *Zambia*

*National Conservation Strategy and
National Environmental Action Plan*

LUBINDA AONGOLA, MINISTRY OF ENVI-
RONMENT AND NATURAL RESOURCES;
STEPHEN BASS, INTERNATIONAL
INSTITUTE FOR ENVIRONMENT AND
DEVELOPMENT (IIED); AND PATRICK
CHIPUNGU, NATIONAL PARKS AND
WILDLIFE SERVICE

**Estimated population 1992:** 8.7 million;
**Land area:** 743,000 km²; **Ecological
zones:** plateau with almost uniform
surface, 1000–1500 metres above sea
level; **Climate:** sub-equatorial, with three
distinct seasons; **Annual rainfall:** 840 mm
at Lusaka; **Forest and woodland area:**
286,800 km²; **GNP per capita:** US$370;
**Main industries:** copper, cobalt, mining;
**ODA received per capita:** US$90.80;
**Population growth rate** (1992–2000):
2.7 per cent; **Life expectancy at birth:**
48.9 years; **Adult literacy rate:** 75.2 per
cent; **Access to safe water:** 53 per cent;
**Access to health services:** 75 per cent;
**Access to sanitation:** 37 per cent

## 1  Introduction

Zambia's environmental management strategy consists of two independently but closely linked strategies: the NCS and the NEAP. The Zambia National Conservation Strategy was the first NCS process in Africa to produce a strategy document and one of the first to receive IUCN technical assistance. This was to a considerable extent the result of presidential support and the involvement of former President Kaunda in the launching of the WCS in 1980. Completed in August 1984, the Zambia NCS document was approved by the Cabinet in July 1985. A linear process has been followed with implementation beginning immediately after the approval of the strategy document with the funding of small demonstration projects followed by substantial institutional and legislative changes in 1989 and 1990. The NEAP is an attempt to review the NCS in order to update Zambia's environmental policies and strategies and keep them alive.

### The NCS

The Zambia NCS process illustrates the value of following an approach which strengthens local skills and institutions. Developed largely by Zambians, with full political support from the President, the NCS process in Zambia acted as a catalyst for local environmental and development activities. The early implementation of many NCS projects provided training opportunities which helped create a core of Zambians who have sustained the NCS process through a decade fraught with economic crises and natural hardships. NCS implementation activities also created momentum which led to the establishment of a number of key environmental institutions and legislative reforms, including the establishment of the Environment Council of Zambia.

In the early 1980s there were no other strategy processes to copy or learn from. The Zambia NCS had to be creative and innovative. It must therefore be considered a pilot strategy in terms of technical input, participation and political support. Produced before the concepts of sustainable development and environmental economics were widely accepted and understood, the Zambia NCS recognized the necessary links that must be built with the economic and development planning system. This feature has remained a key positive element in the ongoing implementation of the Zambia NCS.

At times the strategic focus of the NCS was sacrificed in favour of securing funding and undertaking projects which were of interest to donors, but did not necessarily further the goals of the NCS. In addition, the size of the Secretariat was initially too small to adequately handle the wide range of NCS activities. As a result, technical input from the social sciences, as well as skills in the areas of participatory methods and communications, were missing in the Secretariat.

However, it is impressive that a decade after the start of the NCS process in Zambia, despite increasing economic constraints, changing political regimes and a highly mobile professional population, the core of Zambians involved in the NCS process has remained both committed to and involved in environment and development matters in Zambia.

### The NEAP

The NEAP was designed to build on the strength of the NCS and address its shortcomings as a strategy for sustainable development. Therefore, the NEAP was to develop the NCS into specific action plans, projects and programmes, forming a kind of NCS/NEAP symbiosis. In so doing, care had to be taken in order to ensure that the NEAP did not become excessively oriented toward conservation, given the bias of the NCS. A balance between conservation needs and socio-economic needs had to be achieved. This was sought by identification of priority environmental problems using clearly defined scientific criteria on the one hand and discussions with stakeholders on the other.

Like the NCS process, however, the NEAP had significant difficulties in addressing these environmental issues in the necessary cross-sectoral way. Probably the most important characteristic of the NEAP process has been the efforts to ensure that the resultant policy framework is consistent with that of the overall national economic policy. Thus, the NEAP had to provide for new opportunities for the involvement of the private sector and the communities in the management of the environment, while at the same time recognizing the increased role for government in monitoring, regulation and enforcement of appropriate resource uses in the interest of sustainable development.

## 2 Scope and Objectives

The overall goal of the NCS process, as stated in the strategy document, is to 'satisfy the basic needs of all the people of Zambia, both present and future generations, through the wise management of natural resources'.

The objectives of the NCS are to:

- ensure the sustainable use of Zambia's renewable natural resources;
- maintain Zambia's biological diversity; and
- maintain essential ecological processes and life-support systems.

It is noteworthy that the overall goal of the NCS is a social one, while the NCS process concentrated on the environmental and resource management aspects of development. This emphasis was due in part to the dominant 'conservation for development' ethic of the 1980 World Conservation Strategy. In the NCS document much attention was paid to development threats to the environment, and also to natural resource potentials for development. The strategy document's analysis was organized around development sectors such as agriculture, fisheries, mining and industry, and their implications for conservation. Social aspects in the strategy received scant attention in spite of the NCS's overall social goal. This was partly due to a lack of NCS participants with specific training in social sciences. The population issue was recognized as important, however, principally in terms of the growing aggregate demand for resources and the likely environmental and health consequences, rather than aspects of equity and participation.

A further consequence of the emphasis on 'conservation for development' planning was that biodiversity and wildlife issues were given little attention in the NCS document. This was a result of a deliberate attempt to elevate the profile of the NCS above the then politically inconsequential wildlife sector (this has since changed), and place it closer to planning and finance interests. The

message 'conservation is much more than wildlife preservation' was effectively transmitted, although it did little to help the important wildlife sector, or encourage new ways of looking at the biodiversity of Zambia.

Cross-sectoral functions such as legislation, education, extension, organization and planning formed the bulk of the prescriptions in the strategy document. This approach offered effective interdisciplinary ways of bringing sectors together, to maximize cross-sectoral synergies and to minimize antagonisms. It ensured that every sector saw the value of, and had appropriate means for, coordinating with other sectors rather than carrying on separately as before.

Economic issues were covered under financial policy. In this, there was a presumption that most of the costs of the NCS would be borne by the government. There were some general statements about resource pricing reflecting externalities, and other environmental economics principles that were not usually included at the time. This occurred several years before the ascendancy of environmental economics in strategic planning. However, there were few tangible provisions in the strategy document concerning economic incentives and the limitations of market mechanisms. There was almost no cost-benefit analysis of the strategy prescriptions, in spite of the various statements of how the NCS would reduce the government's financial burden.

In contrast, the main objective of the NEAP is to review and integrate environmental concerns into the social and economic development process of the country, ensuring that it is consistent with the country's new market economy orientation. The NEAP process was undertaken within the framework of three guiding principles, namely:

- Zambian citizens have a right to a clean and healthy environment;
- there is a need to have broad community and private sector participation in policy formulation and implementation; and
- all major development projects should be subject to EIAs.

## 3 Relationship to Development Planning

The need for close links with the development planning system was fully recognized by the participants of both the NCS and the NEAP processes. Critical to the development of any strategies for sustainable development is the integration of such a strategy in overall national development plans. Even though this aspect is essential, it has been one of the most difficult to achieve for the Zambian strategy.

The National Commission for Development Planning (NCDP) was encouraged to participate in both the NCS and the NEAP, although in reality the Ministry of Lands and Natural Resources (later the Ministry of Environment and Natural Resources) has remained the more active partner in both processes. There was an initial tendency on the part of the economic planning system to regard the NCS and the NEAP processes as potentially costly encumbrances. However, this fear has faded over time and there has been an increased involvement by NCDP in the NEAP process. In addition, there has been a realization by economists of the value of the natural resources of Zambia and of the need for EIAs in order to obtain donor funding.

Key aspects of the NCS Strategy have been implemented through NCDP, notably the environmental assessment programme initiated in 1986. This programme was designed to help NCDP integrate environmental assessments into the government project appraisal cycle, and to build the principles of environmental economics into the development planning system. NCDP remains an interested partner in integrating environmental economics into the Public Investment Programme (which is part of the structural adjustment programme) and in building environmental assessment criteria into its project appraisal cycle.

With respect to the NEAP process, the critical question posed by several parties concerns the role played in the process by the central economic planning agency, the NCDP. The argument is that the NEAP process can only achieve its goal of integrating environmental considerations in the overall social and economic development goal if NCDP plays a key role in this process. However, it has not been possible to get NCDP to play a significant role, apart from being represented by interested individual staff members at the planning and technical committee and task force levels. In addition, with the public sector reform process still underway there are doubts about how overall planning and coordination will be addressed in the future.

## 4 Initial Development

### NCS Start-Up

The NCS was initiated in October 1980 by Kenneth Kaunda, former President of Zambia. He was one of many heads of state who simultaneously launched the World Conservation Strategy in capital cities throughout the world. Assistance in preparing an NCS was requested from IUCN through its Director General, who was visiting the country at the time of the launch.

In deciding on the focus for the Zambia NCS, a significant factor was the establishment of IUCN's Conservation for Development Centre (CDC), with its priority of reorienting national development policy and planning processes towards what was becoming known as sustainable development. CDC provided technical assistance for this purpose to governments in developing countries. In Zambia an IUCN consultant assisted during the preparation of the strategy document for a period of six months; later, several long-term consultants assisted during the NCS approval and early implementation phases and acted as secretaries of the National Conservation Committee, a precursor to the eventual Environment Council of Zambia.

The Ministry of Lands and Natural Resources (MLNR) was nominated as the central body for coordinating the NCS. The NCDP, however, as the body with a mandate to coordinate development planning across all sectors, was encouraged to take an equal part in the NCS work. Theoretically NCDP was the principal leverage point for integrating conservation into the development process in Zambia.

Unfortunately, the relationship between these two government bodies was not smooth. The MLNR saw the NCS as a principal means of raising its policy profile and ensuring that the work of more prominent ministries was environmentally sound. In contrast, the NCDP saw the NCS, at least in the first few years, as a potentially complicated hindrance in what was, at the time, an overburdened and somewhat confused central planning system. It is notable that the MLNR and its successor, the Ministry of Environment and Natural Resources (MENR) and the Environment Council of Zambia have remained the focal point for the NCS and the NEAP, with the NCDP playing a secondary role.

### The NEAP

Although design and implementation of projects under the auspices of the NCS was still going on even in the early 1990s, it was felt that there was a need to update Zambia's environmental policy and translate it into tangible improvements in human livelihood. The most important external stimulus to this was the Agenda 21 guidelines adopted at the 1992 United Nations Conference on Environment and Development (UNCED). Among the possible alternatives available for updating the NCS, MENR favoured the NEAP process since it would also enable the government to fulfil the World Bank's criteria to continue to benefit from the Bank's IDA loan facility.

In July 1992, MENR formally requested financial and technical assistance from the World Bank for the preparation of an NEAP. In October 1992, the World Bank sent a mission to discuss the preparation of an NEAP with senior officials of the Zambian Government, donors and other key individuals, and to seek agreement with the government on how to develop the Zambian NEAP. The extent to which the ministry held consultations before requesting World Bank assistance cannot be established. One thing is clear, however; the Environmental Council of Zambia, which had already constituted a committee to oversee the updating of the NCS with the assistance of IUCN, was not consulted.

At the consultation meetings with the Bank, two Permanent Secretaries who were members of the Environment Council expressed their pessimism about the NEAP, given that there was already an NCS document. The World Bank delegation assured the meeting that the process would seek to augment and strengthen existing institutional arrangements, studies and information, particularly the NCS. The delegation further assured the meeting that the Bank would not dictate to the government but would assist in identifying those areas in which the country needed help. By implication this meant that the Bank could support a Government of Zambia/ IUCN initiative of updating the NCS. In terms of strengths and weaknesses, such an initiative was more acceptable. It was feared, however, that the Bank might not agree that the initiative would meet the conditions to obtain IDA funds, and that further demands would be made on Zambia.

## 5 Preparation and Participation

### The NCS

The NCS process was initially housed in MLNR. Two key groups were formed to develop the NCS: a task force, or policy review group; and a Technical Group.

The NCS was served by a small full-time Secretariat to undertake day-to-day planning, review, editing and rationalizing of the various products of the Technical Group. In retrospect, the Secretariat was too small in size and narrow in skills to adequately handle the full range of NCS development, implementation and administrative activities.

The Task Force, which made executive decisions on the direction and administration of the NCS, was made up of 15 Zambians at senior levels. These were principally government officers, from departmental director to permanent secretary level, but also included representatives from selected parastatals, the University of Zambia, the political party (Zambia was then a one-party state) and one conservation NGO.

Meeting monthly, this group commissioned special studies, reviewed the policy implications of these studies, and ensured that the final strategy was well-balanced for presentation to Cabinet by the Minister of LNR. The work clearly captured the interest of the Task Force, with the result that few dropped out of the process, and there was very little delegation of work to junior officers.

The Technical Group conducted background studies and discussed technical issues in a number of smaller working groups. These groups comprised 30 respected professionals (70 per cent of whom were Zambians) from a range of institutions similar to those represented on the Task Force, with a few knowledgeable expatriates working on relevant activities in Zambia.

The papers produced by the Technical Group generally focused on issues related to natural resource use, such as charcoal burning and deforestation, water pollution resulting from increasing squatter settlements, and so on. An excellent response was achieved: 29 out of 30 background papers were prepared within six weeks, with no incentive other than personal involvement in a worthwhile process. The advantage of the short timeframe was that the main issues came to the surface quickly, with little time for procrastination. The disadvantages were that some of the analysis in the technical papers was not very substantial, some data was outdated, and in some cases the analysis was wrong.

Following the background papers, Technical Group seminars were held to define the priority issues in each sector, identify common issues across sectors, and then to develop sectoral and cross-sectoral options for dealing with the issues. There were no particularly rigorous methods for determining priorities, other than the technical and political consensus reached by the Technical Group and Task Force, respectively. Task Force seminars were held to review the work of the Technical Group, particularly the policy implications, and to decide on further analysis or the choice of options.

During the process, a broad cross-section of mainly government and parastatal interests, together with the University of Zambia and the National Council for Scientific Research, took part in the development of the strategy document. A growing body of conservation NGOs and interest groups also became involved. The private business sector was not involved, with the exception of representation from the Commercial Farmers' Bureau.

Participation among the members of the NCS Task Force and Technical Group was highly active and fruitful. In general, however, the strategy preparation process was basically one of consultation amongst government technocrats and administrators, with some technical guidance from IUCN, and technical inputs and advocacy from the NGOs. There was no comprehensive public participation programme for several reasons:

- a presumption that Zambia's relatively decentralized and democratic system of government would take care of the 'local needs' aspects of the NCS;
- a lack of scientists and economists outside government (especially with skills in environmental areas);
- a very small private business sector, since most major industrial and commercial bodies were government-controlled parastatals;
- a weak NGO sector, especially environmental NGOs (wildlife groups, many of which emphasized anti-poaching activities, did not represent local community interests, and although the social sector NGOs were relatively strong, and closer to the grassroots, the NCS did not see the value of capturing their inputs) with the exception of one NGO, Human Settlements of Zambia (HUZA), which specializes in housing and resettlement issues;
- at the time the general approach of aid-funded national policy studies did not seek to involve more than government and a few special-interest NGOs; and
- the lack of a tradition of full public participation in policy formulation in Zambia.

Nonetheless, the NCS document preparation was one of the first activities in Zambia to capture some of the inputs of NGOs and parastatals in formulating broad policy. Furthermore, the non-government bodies selected were carefully chosen as being highly relevant to the policies under discussion. They included, for example, the National Council for Scientific Research, the university, the Commercial Farmers Bureau, Zambia Consolidated Copper Mines, and HUZA.

One particularly successful tactical move in the NCS preparation was the involvement of the media. Care was taken to communicate the issues identified by the NCS process and their solutions, through newspapers, radio and television. Journalists found considerable substance in the NCS process and many stories were produced that brought the issues closer to the public.

Inadvertently, the media acted as a feedback mechanism for those involved in the process. The media provided not only public opinion on issues, but also made it clear to the Technical Group and Task Force that they were dealing with issues that were real and important to the general public. This media contact, and a well-executed educational campaign through posters and displays in schools and government offices all over the country, constituted the communications work during NCS preparation. However

the full potential of this communications work to elicit feedback from the public was not developed.

During the process, three drafts of the NCS document were prepared before submission to Cabinet. For expediency, it was agreed that the Secretariat would actually write the strategy, based closely on inputs outlined by the Task Force. The Cabinet's advisors took 12 months to review the institutional, legal and budgetary consequences of the NCS before Cabinet approved it in July 1985. The final published strategy document includes some amendments by the Cabinet, notably putting more of the institutional burden back on the MLNR than on the Task Force.

Part of the intention of the strategy document was to influence donors to ensure that aid policies and practices were environmentally sound, and to attract additional support for the chronically underfunded environmental multiple resource use sectors. Hence there was a focus on projects and the environmental assessment of project impacts, which was felt to be instructive for donors and help focus their development assistance.

In the period between the finalisation and approval of the strategy document the Natural Resources Development Plan was prepared. This included about 20 environmental, natural resource and urban improvement projects designed for development assistance. In retrospect, to structure this Investment Plan, as it was also known, to be donor-dependent was not a sound move towards sustainability. However, it was inspired by three factors: the perceived need to demonstrate to the Zambian government that the NCS was important and could attract donor funding; the recognition that, as a result of government neglect of environmental matters, there was a need for some basic investment in environmental management; and a need for IUCN to generate funds through projects to continue offering technical assistance to Zambia.

### The NEAP

In many respects the methodology used for the preparation of the NEAP is similar to that used for the preparation of the NCS. Unlike the NCS, however, which received a lot of political support, the Cabinet-level Environment and Natural Resources Development Committee (ENRDC), which was to provide policy direction and assure full governmental participation in the NEAP process, only met twice, early in the process before issue papers were prepared. Therefore, the NEAP process did not actually benefit from the political input of the government.

The NEAP Planning and Technical Committee (PTC), with representatives of relevant line ministries, research and academic institutions, the private sector and NGOs, was appointed by the Minister of Environment and Natural Resources. The PTC determined the task forces, which consisted of three to six members drawn from the organizations represented in the PTC, chaired by a PTC member. The task force areas of responsibility were chosen bearing in mind those successfully used by the NCS. This ensured that the symbiosis between the NCS and NEAP was kept alive with respect to the structure. The difference lay at the political level, however.

At the consultative stage it was generally agreed that in carrying out their work, the NEAP Task Forces would establish contacts with local resource users, preferably down to the district or even village level, so as to ensure broad participation in the review process and prescription of actions required. However, the task forces carried out desk-based literature searches and no consultations were carried out. The main constraint to wider participation was the time factor. The time allocated for the preparation of the background papers was not enough to enable wider consultations. Further, facilitation of participation of the local people requires application of relevant methodologies, with which most of the task force members might not have been familiar.

The location of the NEAP Secretariat within the relatively new ministry, and outside the well established institutions such as the NCDP or the Environmental Council of Zambia, led to some serious start-up problems which slowed down the process. For example, the work of the Secretariat was greatly affected by lack of office accommodation which raised questions about the government's commitment to the process. Had the Secretariat been based in the Environmental Council, office space would not have been a problem. Further, the Secretariat would have benefited greatly from the technical staff at the Council. Meanwhile, there was no technical staff at the ministry headquarters although the idea of a Planning Department had been accepted and was awaiting Cabinet approval. Despite the ministry's frantic efforts to create an informal Planning Unit, it became difficult for it to provide significant support given the location of the Coordinator in an office away from the ministry.

The status of the NEAP Coordinator also created problems. Although it had been agreed that a person appointed as full time NEAP Coordinator should be a Zambian of standing so that it would be easy for him/her to work with senior policy makers and the international community supporting the NEAP, this was not followed through. This seems to have undermined the status of the NEAP as a

multi-sector programme, although the NEAP-PTC, with its 17 high level members, did assist the Coordinator in the effective management of the process.

Despite these various problems, the draft NEAP policy document was compiled by the core group of the PTC from the issue papers prepared by the task forces. The papers were first scrutinized by a sub-committee of the PTC and other experts from the relevant fields. The initial plan was to take the draft document to regional or provincial seminars to ensure a broad input of views. However, as the NEAP had to be prepared in only nine months (from October 1993 to June 1994) it was realized that it was not possible for the provincial workshops to await the draft document. Therefore, it was decided that provincial seminars could still go ahead with the objectives of preparing Regional Environmental Action Plans (REAPs) and investment programmes. The REAPs enlisted support of local communities in identifying local environmental problems, their causes and solutions and contributed a separate section to the NEAP.

The PTC took advantage of the broad coverage of the Zambia Environmental Education Programme (ZEEP), an NGO, and appointed it to manage the provincial workshops. ZEEP successfully conducted provincial workshops across the country and compiled REAP reports. The workshops were attended by representatives from government, private institutions, NGOs, community-based organizations, and traditional, religious and civic leaders. Each workshop was observed by a member of the PTC. Unlike the NCS, the NEAP went beyond mere consultation amongst government technocrats and administrators but included the civil society in the rural areas.

### *Donor Support and Participation*

The NCS process was supported financially by the Swedish and Dutch governments, although some other donors were also involved. However, donor support was focused on a series of short projects with rigid objectives and deadlines that tended to compromise the flexibility and quality of the NCS process. In the preparation stage of the NCS document, this inevitably put an inappropriate emphasis on report deadlines. Donor support for the preparation of the NEAP has come from the World Bank, UNDP and NORAD. Continued implementation of the NCS has been facilitated by funding from donors, such as CIDA and SIDA, largely for institutional strengthening. Again, the pressure of the IDA's June 1994 deadline caused the NEAP to be prepared with little room for flexibility.

### *Monitoring and Evaluation*

There was no internal monitoring or evaluation of the Zambia NCS. SIDA did

review the progress of the NCS regularly in line with their contract with IUCN and the Zambian government. There was no element of internal monitoring and evaluation in the NEAP either. Lack of this element can be attributed to the fact that the NEAP's imperative was largely seen in the sense of delivering a number of bankable projects for presentation to donors and not in the resulting processes of decision-making, participation and capacity-building. The World Bank performed its own monitoring, however, by sending mission after mission to ensure that the process was on course to advise the government accordingly.

## *6 Results and Implementation*

### *NCS*

The Zambia NCS is notable for its early implementation of projects during the preparation of the actual strategy document, while waiting for approval of the strategy and after adoption by Cabinet. This early implementation served to generate both a core of Zambians experienced in various environmental fields, as well as a momentum for the NCS which has been maintained throughout the decade. In addition, following approval of the NCS document, elements in it were incorporated in the fourth Five-Year Plan which was then being finalized.

The NCS Secretariat and task force continued for four years in a similar working style to that during the preparation of the strategy. The task force served as a National Conservation Committee (NCC), an interim authority prior to the appointment of the Environment Council of Zambia (ECZ) in 1990. However, the NCC suffered from having no power except that which could be exercised by its individual members through their own ministries or organizations. Hence a voluntary approach, rather than a regulatory approach, came to characterize the NCC's progress from 1985 to 1990. A legislative mandate was not obtained until the creation of the Environment Council of Zambia through enactment of the Environmental Protection and Pollution Control Act of 1990.

In the year between completion of the NCS document and Cabinet approval, the Task Force and Secretariat generated specific activities to implement the draft NCS principles. In the interim, while the major institutional and procedural changes awaited approval by Cabinet and adoption by Parliament, implementation focused on two localities with very different circumstances and needs.

The first project focused on integrating natural resource initiatives such as urban forestry and improved charcoal stoves into a squatter upgrading project run by HUZA in Lusaka. It was initially successful as a low-key, low-budget activity, but slowly faded out after four years because the NCS did not have the skills or resources with which to support such participatory projects.

The second activity was in a marginal rural area where traditional, high-input agriculture was not possible or desirable, but where new uses of local resources might be sustained. The NCS, along with others, encouraged community wildlife utilization and multiple land use in the Luangwa Valley. This project eventually became the Luangwa Integrated Resource Development Project, a far bigger project than envisaged in the NCS, employing many MLNR and NCDP resources (to the detriment of other NCS projects in need of scarce human resources and financial assistance).

After approval of the strategy document, an extremely wide range of activities ensued, such as the establishment of a Natural Resources Data Bank, the nomination of Victoria Falls as a World Heritage Site, EIAs, training in EIAs, and soil conservation research. In effect, this was implementation of elements of the Natural Resources Development Plan. The search for donor funding for these activities led to a project-based approach with relatively short time horizons. Although the various projects all had to be justified to the NCC as to their strategic importance, this was an extremely opportunistic phase. The interests of donors and the availability of funding had a strong influence on the course of NCS implementation. As a result, although all the projects had their origins in the NCS document, the process lost its strategic focus.

The major reform of legislation and a coordinating organization recommended in the strategy document made slow progress through government from 1986 to 1989. It was hindered in part by an early draft environmental protection and pollution control act which had been making its way through the judicial system and finally surfaced as a bill at the same time as the NCS's Environment Protection and Pollution Control Bill. Progress may also have been hindered by the NCS's emphasis on projects which, by prevailing standards in Zambia, were appearing fast and furious and tackling real needs in an efficient and pragmatic way without any institutional change. Even though environmental legislation and environmental institutions were needed in Zambia to sustain long-term change, the emphasis on projects may have deflected attention from the need for institutional and legislative reform.

Such reform finally came about with the enactment of the Environmental Protection and Pollution Control Act of 1990, which created the ECZ. Appointments to the ECZ largely involved senior government officials along with several private sector and NGO interests. Many members of the ECZ are the original NCS Task Force and National Conservation Committee members of almost a decade, providing continuity and commitment to the continued implementation of the NCS process.

Within the structure of the ECZ there is a Secretariat and a number of Pollution Control Inspectorates for air, water, noise and radiation, with the power to set and enforce standards for emissions and effluent discharge. The ECZ is seen to be one of the most progressive environmental institutions in Africa today, with wide-ranging powers to provide advice to the government on all matters related to environment, to carry out research, and to establish and enforce pollution control measures.

In addition to the ECZ, a Ministry of Environment and Natural Resources was created in 1990 to replace the former Ministry of Lands and Natural Resources. This ministry works with the ECZ in response to the policy advice of the Council, and provides environmental assessment and planning services to other line ministries involved with resource management. A clear distinction between the role of the ECZ and the new Ministry of Environment and Natural Resources has yet to develop within the Zambian government.

One recent area of initiative stemming from the NCS is the preparation of an Environmental Planning Programme for Zambia. This includes the development of Environmental Assessment capacity for the Environmental Council of Zambia and an environmental economics programme for NCDP. This is linked to the recent establishment of an Environmental Planning Unit for MENR.

*Results of the Strategy*

Despite the fact that the Zambia NCS was one of the first conservation strategies in Africa, and had to make its way through relatively uncharted waters, it has achieved a great deal over the past decade. In terms of legislative and institutional change it has produced some of the most progressive environmental legislation and institutional development in Africa today. In addition, it has remained closely linked with the National Commission for Development Planning which, although it has not led the way in NCS implementation, has remained involved in and supportive of the strategy.

The NCS process has contributed greatly to capacity-building in Zambia through the many projects it has spawned in the fields of environmental assessment and planning, protected-area management, forestry, wetlands management, community wildlife utilization, resettlement and pollution control. Although some of these projects may have been opportunistic and lacking in strategic focus, they have given Zambians considerable field experience in environmental projects, and have built up a core of increasingly skilled environmental professionals.

Perhaps one of the most impressive results of the NCS process is the continued existence of the core of committed Zambians who first formed the NCS Task Force and Conservation Committee and who, a decade later, remain enthusiastic supporters for continued implementation of NCS activities. Through a severe economic decline, a change of government and the worst drought of the century, many of the original NCS supporters remain involved in promoting an updated NCS and an environmental action plan.

*Outcome of the NEAP Process*

The main outcome of the NEAP process is an NEAP policy document that reflects the country's major environmental concerns, identifies the principal causes of the environmental problems, and formulates policies and actions to deal with them. This document, adopted by the government in December 1994, includes a number of important elements. These are:

• a list of major environmental issues that must be tackled;

- an analysis of major cross-sectoral issues and socio-economic factors important to environmental management;
- a detailed legal and institutional framework review;
- an assessment of information needs in all sectors;
- recommendations for specific action in each sector, giving priority, timing and institutional responsibilities; and
- recommendations for an overall strategy, giving priority actions.

Unlike the NCS, the NEAP document was accompanied by the REAP, which outlined environmental problems in the nine provinces and the actions required. The NEAP policy document will be implemented through a compendium of bankable investment projects known as the Environmental Support Programme (ESP) which is now being developed. The preparation of the ESP, which is the second outcome of the NEAP process, started even before the NEAP policy document was adopted in December 1994. It began with a training workshop for selected experts and preceded the national workshop that reviewed the draft NEAP policy document. The training workshop participants were drawn from government, NGOs and the private sector. Although the preparation of the ESP was supposed to be complete by July 1995, operational difficulties made it difficult to meet this deadline.

The third outcome of the NEAP process is increased public awareness and training. A number of workshops, involving people from all walks of life, have been convened to achieve this. Through the exchange of ideas a number of people, including those who are not experts in the environment, have been exposed to environmental issues affecting the country.

The fourth outcome of the NEAP process is capacity-building at ZEEP and MENR. ZEEP, which normally deals with environmental education in primary schools, was given the task of conducting provincial workshops. Through this arrangement the organization was able to build capacity outside its normal areas of operation.

## 7  Lessons Learned

*NCS: Factors that promoted the strategy*

**Strong political support:** the WCS launch, as an international political event, invited a significant policy response from the Zambian government, with personal interest from the President and other high-level officials.

**Local capacity-building and ownership:** IUCN's vision of NCSs and provision of technical assistance focused on strengthening local skills and initiatives, allowing Zambia to develop a strong 'made in Zambia' strategy which has endured well.

**Consensus:** partly because the NCS process involved a small and manageable group of senior government officials and key decision-makers, it was possible to achieve a consensus on key issues.

**Staffing:** MLNR seconded an excellent counterpart for the Secretariat, an individual with a broad understanding of cross-cutting issues and unrestrained by hierarchies and divisions. The IUCN expatriate advisor was skilled at capacity-building and worked well with his counterparts throughout the process, transferring technical knowledge and building an atmosphere of trust and respect within the team.

**Creativity:** the exploratory nature of the work favoured a creative approach (there were no other NCSs to 'copy').

**Lack of competition and political risk:** there were no competing projects or studies with similar national cross-sectoral scopes. 'Environment' was not yet perceived in Zambia as a politically contentious issue, and so was not treated with undue political caution. Hence participants were free to conduct their inquiries unconstrainedly. Social and economic issues were contentious, however; even if the NCS had set out to address them directly, it might not have been successful.

**Recognition of the importance of renewable natural resources:** copper prices had been declining for some years, Zambians realized that a continuing 90 plus per cent dependence upon copper exports was unsustainable, and that its renewable natural resources held much unrealized potential. At the time when the NCS process started, there was a major 'back-to-the-land' political campaign to try and reverse the trend towards increasing urbanization and it may be that the NCS seemed to offer ways to achieve this.

**Lack of cost–benefit analysis:** the fact that the NCS document had not really examined the costs and benefits of recommendations aided its approval, albeit inappropriately. Today it is a different story: the costs of NCS (and NEAP) implementation are all too clear, and it is obvious that the win-win promise of the NCS cannot entirely be kept.

**Accessible documentation for Cabinet:** the short time available for NCS preparation ensured that only the most immediately obvious issues were put to Cabinet. This avoided the possibility of creating an enormous agenda which Cabinet may have found difficult to consider.

**Political and technical support:** strong political support, along with support from technical and senior administrative staff in government, was essential for ensuring the long-term momentum and enthusiasm for NCS activities, long after external assistance ended.

*Factors that hindered the strategy*

**New concepts:** the concepts of 'conservation for development' and 'sustainable development' were not yet widely known. There was therefore a great deal of work involved, principally by the Secretariat, just to discuss basic concepts with members of the Task Force and the Technical Group as well as the wider public.

**Restrictions:** in retrospect, the WCS may have been too restrictive in the preparation of national objectives, especially given the lack of social and economic skills among the NCS participants.

**Lack of technical skills:** having initiated a strategy process in Zambia, IUCN left it almost entirely alone. Hence the range of IUCN skills that had been made available to the WCS was not available for the Zambia NCS, despite the latter being a critical test of the WCS. (This isolation did ensure, however, that the NCS was very much a Zambian product.) There were inadequate skills in Zambia for policy analysis, especially for cross-cutting issues. The tradition of policy analysis was very sectoral. Other skill shortages that resulted in compromising quality were the lack of Secretariat skills in the social sciences, public participation, resource economics and communications.

**Shortage of time and resources:** the discontinuous project approach meant that there wasn't enough time or resources to elaborate an adequate number of options, to subject them to rigorous priority setting exercises, or to discuss them thoroughly. There was enough time (six months) to get through all the tasks, but not enough for the necessary reflection and refinement of the analysis.

**Lack of strategic approach:** the NCS proved to be good at adding initiatives, but weak at eliminating anomalous or inappropriate ones. In this sense, it was not an adequate strategic tool. The need to be strategic in implementing activities and projects should have been given more attention. In wishing to attract and keep donor interest, the Zambia NCS was, at times, too opportunistic and occasionally lost sight of the overall role of projects.

**Other factors:** weaknesses in the implementation of the strategy were due to a lack of resources and skills to ensure sustainability of field projects, lack of a broad base of public support beyond the government officials, private sector individuals and NGOs involved in the process, and a lack of strategic influence over major economic policies related to structural adjustment (such an influence being a tall order in any country).

**Over-burdening of the Secretariat:** the Zambia NCS Secretariat recognized in retrospect that they could have benefited from additional staff with skills in the social sciences field, along with assistance with public participation and communications aspects of the strategy. They simply could not do everything that was required to develop, implement and administer a successful NCS.

**Lack of links to development planning:** even though the Zambia NCS process has recognized the value of a close partnership with development planning and economic planning institutions, this relationship has not been fully developed to achieve the maximum benefits. NCDP has not become as fully involved in the NCS as MENR, and consequently economic policies have not been reformed as the NCS document recommended.

*NEAP: Factors that Promoted the Plan*

The main strengths of the Zambian NEAP are:

- the need to update the NCS was a demand-driven in-country process, although there was little or no consultation on the model of the NEAP preparation;
- participation in the NEAP process was broader than for the NCS and included other stakeholders;
- the NEAP process was built on existing data and strategies, ie the NCS;
- the NEAP process was supported by a

rigorous economic and social analysis of major environmental issues; and
- the NEAP process increased environmental awareness to a cross-section of Zambian people.

*Weaknesses*

The main weaknesses were:

- the imperative to produce a number of bankable projects distorted the process and may lead to the loss of strategic integrity and focus and an increased dependence on external finance;
- the process lacked high-level political support;
- participation in the process was not broad enough;
- integration of the NEAP process into the main stream economic development planning has proved difficult;
- the NEAP document did not include a work plan or budgetary implications of implementing the policy;
- the NEAP document failed to prioritize environmental problems; and
- lack of monitoring and evaluation systems, including methods, skills and processes, which are needed to assess progress in the development and implementation of sustainable development strategies.

## 8 Conclusions

A number of lessons have been learned in the process of developing and implementing the NCS and the NEAP in Zambia. The most important one is that there should be a clear vision of what a country wants to achieve before undertaking a process of developing a strategy like an NCS or NEAP. This means that donors should only serve to assist in the process, not lead in terms of deciding what should be achieved. In the case of Zambia, a clear vision would have assisted in setting up a realistic time frame for the NEAP process that would have allowed for broad public participation. A clear vision would also have reduced the institutional conflicts that were brought by the institutional framework established for the NEAP process. In other words, there was no need to create a separate secretariat when one could have been housed in the Environmental Council of Zambia.

## 9  *Chronology*

1980    WCS launched. Kenneth Kaunda, former President of Zambia, launched the WCS. Lee Talbot, Director General of IUCN, accompanied Dr Kaunda in Lusaka on that occasion. Kaunda, a wildlife enthusiast, suggested that Zambia prepare a national response to the WCS, and requested IUCN's assistance.

1983    Two IUCN consultancies carried out a feasibility study for a Zambia NCS, and a prospectus for an NCS was prepared.

1984    Provision of an IUCN consultant to the Ministry of Lands and Natural Resources for a six-month period for the preparation of an NCS document. Creation of the NCS Secretariat. Completion of the NCS in August 1984.

1985    Approval of the NCS by Cabinet. The task force becomes the National Conservation Committee and continues until the establishment of the ECZ. NCS demonstration projects begin with a squatter upgrading project carried out by HUZA, and NCS support to the establishment of the Luangwa Integrated Rural Development Project (LIRDP) in the Luangwa Valley.

1986    Provision of IUCN technical assistance to the NCS Secretariat to assist with the implementation of the NCS from February 1985 to September 1986. Preparation of the Natural Resources Development Plan containing 20 environmental, natural resources and urban improvement projects to act as an Investment Plan for the NCS and to get an early start on implementation of the NCS through donor supported projects.

1988    Creation of the NCS Task Force and Technical Working Groups to prepare the NCS and oversee the implementation of projects. Establishment of the School of Environmental Studies at the Copperbelt University.

1989    Additional part-time secondments of GRZ staff from the Department of Town and Country Planning, NCDP, and MLNR. Additional IUCN technical assistance on project specific activities, such as environmental impact assessments. Provision of an IUCN Advisor in EIA to NCDP to carry out training in environmental assessment and resource economics. Establishment of the Natural Resources Data Bank at UNZA; moved to the ECZ in 1992. Establishment of ZEEP. Structural adjustment policies are imposed by the IMF and World Bank; five-year planning system shifts to a system of Public Investment Plans (PIP) and a six-month cycle of economic adjustment.

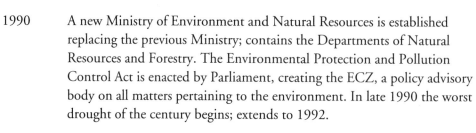

| | |
|---|---|
| 1990 | A new Ministry of Environment and Natural Resources is established replacing the previous Ministry; contains the Departments of Natural Resources and Forestry. The Environmental Protection and Pollution Control Act is enacted by Parliament, creating the ECZ, a policy advisory body on all matters pertaining to the environment. In late 1990 the worst drought of the century begins; extends to 1992. |
| 1991 | End of the Second Republic, one-party state, dominated by the United National Independence Party (UNIP). Start of the Third Republic, with a multi-party system. New government of the Movement for Multi-Party Democracy (MMD) headed by Mr F Chiluba. Caring for the Earth (successor to the WCS) is launched in Lusaka. |
| 1992 | Appointments are made to the ECZ and the Council holds its first meeting. NCS implementation continues with the design of an Environmental Planning Programme in conjunction with IUCN and GRZ. The programme is to contain EIA capacity, an environmental economics programme for NCDP and a planning unit for the Ministry of Environment. ECZ and the Ministry propose to update the NCS to meet current requirements of Agenda 21, structural adjustment policies, and other changing national circumstances.

February: The World Bank informs the Zambian government that it must prepare NEAPs by June 1993 if it is to continue to benefit from the IDA.

July: The Zambian government formally requests the World Bank for financial and technical assistance for the NEAP process.

November: First World Bank Mission to consult with the donor community, government and other interested parties and explain the NEAP process. |
| 1993 | The NEAP process is flagged off and Coordinator, members of PTC and task forces are appointed. Provincial Workshops are held in all the nine provinces. |
| 1994 | February. National Workshop to review the draft NEAP policy document.

July: Draft NEAP and REAP documents are submitted to MENR by PTC.

December: Government approves NEAP document.

Preparation of the ESP begins. The World Bank requires an NEAP for Zambia as a requirement of IDA loan funding. |

# Zimbabwe

*National Conservation Strategy*

MARGARET MUKAHANANA; ART HOOLE,
MINISTRY OF ENVIRONMENT AND
TOURISM; MOSES MONEMO; ELLIOT
MHAKA, DEPARTMENT OF NATURAL
RESOURCES; SAM CHIMBUYA, IUCN

**Estimated population 1992:** 10.5
million; **Land area:** 387,000 km²;
**Ecological zones:** land-locked high
plateau, mountains on eastern border;
**Climate:** subtropical, strongly influenced
by altitude, warm and dry lowlands;
**Annual rainfall:** 400–2000 mm; **Forest
and woodland area:** 190,000 km²; **GNP
per capita:** US$580; **Main industries:**
agriculture, livestock, manufacturing;
**ODA received per capita:** US$39.90;
**Population growth rate** (1992–2000):
2.3 per cent; **Life expectancy at birth:**
53.7 years; **Adult literacy rate:** 83.4 per
cent; **Access to safe water:** 84 per cent;
**Access to health services:** 85 per cent;
**Access to sanitation:** 40 per cent

## 1 Introduction

After a protracted war lasting more than a decade, Zimbabwe achieved independence in 1980. The country was faced with the devastating effects of conflict, combined with serious depletion of natural resources resulting largely from a colonial land tenure system. In 1983, however, inspired by the 1980 World Conservation Strategy, Zimbabwe was one of the first countries in Africa to undertake a National Conservation Strategy process.

The NCS document, 'Zimbabwe's Road to Survival', was prepared in 1986 by the Ministry of Natural Resources and Tourism without any external technical or financial assistance. Published by the Ministry in 1987, the strategy was formally launched by His Excellency, the President of the Republic of Zimbabwe, R G Mugabe.

The strategy document presents a profile of environmental issues which has helped raise awareness on the part of government and the public. It has not, however, led to substantial influence over development policies, legislative or economic reforms. Only some elements of the strategy have been implemented since 1987. This was partly due to the absence of an implementation plan detailing actions and responsibilities and the corresponding lack of financial resources. In post-Independence years government priorities in Zimbabwe were largely focused on rehabilitation and reconstruction of infrastructure, such as schools, roads and hospitals. Although environmental matters were highly relevant to the country's future, they were not high on the government's agenda.

This situation changed substantially with the active participation of Zimbabwe representatives in the process leading up to UNCED. The UNCED process led to the development of Agenda 21 priorities for Zimbabwe, including a renewed effort at implementation of the NCS. With financial support from UNDP and technical support from IUCN, the Government of Zimbabwe embarked on the District Environmental Action Planning Process (DEAP) in 1994 as a way of operationalizing the NCS. DEAPs are currently in preparation in eight pilot districts throughout the country.

Some degree of institutional reform has simultaneously taken place in Zimbabwe, including the creation of a new Ministry of Environment and Tourism and its corresponding Environmental Planning and Coordination Unit. This unit hopes to reactivate the momentum of the NCS process through the preparation of an Implementation Action Plan based on the strategy document. In addition, an extensive legislative review has been carried out with a view towards amendments leading to improved environmental regulation and management.

*Zimbabwe*

*173*

## 2 Scope and Objectives

### National Conservation Strategy (NCS)

The Zimbabwe NCS was intended to be a 'policy blueprint' guiding the conservation and management of natural resources of Zimbabwe. As the first document produced after Independence with an integrated focus on the conservation and management of natural resources, it was also a reference document on conservation issues and a focal point for planners.

The objective of the Zimbabwe NCS was to integrate sustainable resource use with every aspect of the nation's social and economic development, and to rehabilitate degraded resources. The strategy also aimed at ensuring the equitable, productive and sustainable utilization of Zimbabwe's natural resources.

The strategy document contains a brief account of the status of the country's natural resources, an inventory of environmental issues, and an overview of prescriptive measures. The natural resources considered include climate, land, soils and vegetation, water, arable and non-arable land, wildlife and protected areas, forest resources, minerals and energy.

The strategy highlights issues such as population growth, pollution, resource planning, land reform, resettlement, preservation of genetic diversity, urbaniza-tion and industrialization, conservation education and awareness, and environmental monitoring, as well as recommendations for legislative and institutional changes.

### District Environmental Action Plans (DEAPs)

The DEAP initiative was seen by the Government of Zimbabwe as a mechanism to operationalize the NCS at the field level. DEAP is an ongoing strategic environmental action planning and implementation process at the district level. Currently underway in eight pilot districts, DEAP involves all sectors of society – community members and leaders, district councils, NGOs and government officials – in a process involving the following:

- participatory assessments of human and ecosystem well-being from the perspective of resource users and district leaders;
- strategic decision-making in which communities and district councils identify solutions and priorities;
- formulation of District Environment Strategies (DESs); and
- the implementation of demonstration activities.

DEAP recognizes that local people have a wealth of indigenous knowledge upon which they have to depend for their livelihood. The methods and tools used in DEAP are designed to be 'user-driven' so that community members and leaders identify the issues, needs and solutions of relevance to them.

DEAP provides a forum and catalyst for articulating and sharing knowledge with local authorities for use in sustainable development planning and implementation. DEAP tools and methods are designed to integrate technical analysis and information generated within government institutions to strengthen and empower local decision-making. DEAP combines local assessments of ecosystem and human well-being plus trends and forecasts with technical analysis available through national government institutions. The DESs then feed into the development planning system at district, provincial and national level.

The DEAP process aims to do the following:

- empower people at the local level to take action;
- strengthen institutions at district and national levels;
- enhance decentralization of resource management to the primary users, including Agritex, local government, Departments of Health, National Affairs and Education, and Rural District Councils (RDCs);

- support local demonstration of sustainable development practices;
- provide a link for national initiatives such as the NEAP, Biodiversity Action Plans, local Agenda 21, Strategies to Combat Desertification, etc;
- provide a link between social and natural resources activities at the district level;
- conserve natural resources through a sustainable use approach; and
- work towards reduction of environmental degradation through a participatory approach, particularly in communal areas.

It is intended that the DEAP process builds from the ground up, with Ward Environmental Action Plans (WEAPs) and Village Environmental Action Plans (VEAPS) leading to the preparation of Provincial Environmental Action Plans (PEAPs) and later to a National Environmental Action Plan (NEAP). This will ensure that national policy and planning frameworks are informed by local needs.

## 3 Relationship to Development Planning

### The NCS

Although the First and Second Five-Year National Development Plans made specific reference to the NCS strategy document as the blueprint for conservation in Zimbabwe, the strategy process was not developed as an integral part of the existing planning and decision-making system.

The NCS document identified the Ministry of Finance, Economic Planning and Development as a critical institution of government in implementing the strategy. The relevance of the strategy to the economic planning and development process was not recognized at the time, however, and as a result the ministries concerned with economic development activities were not key players in the development of the strategy. It was instead developed by the Ministry of Natural Resources and Tourism.

Because the strategy process remained well outside the main economic and planning system in Zimbabwe, it is not surprising that the strategy has had little effect on major economic policies, structural adjustment or fiscal reform. In general, the strategy has not achieved the main goal of integrating sustainable resource use into the economic planning process and policies of Zimbabwe, nor has it had an impact on development planning. However, renewed efforts are being made to build linkages with the Ministry of Finance and the National Economic Planning Commission and to blend the NCS with the UNCED requirement for a National Agenda 21 and the World Bank

requirement for a National Environmental Action Plan (NEAP).

*The DEAP*

DEAP is intended to be fully integrated into the development planning system at the district level. The Rural District Council (RDC) is the main focal point for the DEAP process at this level. DEAPs will inform the District Development Plans which will then be submitted to the planning commission at the national level.

The DEAP process is distinguished from top-down planning in that it recognizes that development initiatives that exclude primary stakeholders tend to fail. It is a 'user-driven' process which seeks to engage and motivate people in taking action at the local level. This provides a bottom-up basis to link with top-down planning processes such as NEAPS and other requirements for national policy frameworks.

## 4 Initial Development

*Development of the NCS*

Exacerbated by the effects of a prolonged war, environmental degradation in Zimbabwe was evident at Independence in the form of serious erosion of rural lands, deforestation, loss of valuable wildlife species and habitat, and pollution of air and water. Faced with increasing population pressure, especially in communal areas, and an inequitable land tenure system, the government recognized the need for an integrated approach to the management of natural resources. Prior to Independence, resource policies were largely sectoral in nature and did not deal adequately with resource management issues in the communal lands where the majority of Zimbabweans reside.

The Ministry of Natural Resources and Tourism saw the National Conservation Strategy as a means of documenting environmental issues and raising the level of environmental awareness of both government and the public. The key participants in developing the strategy were representatives from the Ministry of Natural Resources and Tourism, the Natural Resources Board, the Department of National Parks and Wildlife, national environmental NGOs, and staff from the University of Zimbabwe.

The strategy was initially developed without financial or technical assistance from bilateral or multi-lateral agencies. More recently UNDP, UNEP, IUCN and NORAD have assisted the Ministry in a reassessment of options for the implementation of the strategy.

In 1983 a committee was formed to begin discussing the need for a National Conservation Strategy. The committee represented natural resource interests from government and NGOs, including representatives from the Department of National Parks and Wildlife, the Natural Resources Board, the Agricultural Rural Development Authority (responsible for the country's largest extension service), the National Conservation Trust (a national environment NGO), representatives from the Zimbabwe Promotion Council and Conference Board, and a public relations consultant.

The strategy document was drafted by members of this committee along with staff from the Ministry of Natural Resources and Tourism. Participation in the development of the strategy document by public and private interests was provided through a national conference in 1985. There the draft was reviewed by representatives from government ministries, conservation NGOs, the University of Zimbabwe, women's NGOs, youth groups and church organizations. A consensus on priority issues was reached in workshops at the conference; this provided guidance to the committee in finalizing the strategy document.

There was limited grassroots participation in preparing the strategy document due to a lack of financial resources, and because rural priorities in post-Independence Zimbabwe were focused not on conservation, but on basic survival needs of health, education and resettlement after a long period of civil war.

After incorporating feedback from the conference, the strategy document was published in 1987 and distributed to conference participants, Members of Parliament, and provincial and district councils.

*Development of the DEAP*

The DEAP process, which started in 1994, relies on the motivation, interest and commitment of villagers, district officers and NGOs. A national representative trains a Core Team of eight district officers from different sectors (natural resources, health, agriculture and forestry) who in turn train the District Strategy Teams. Team members work with villagers, community leaders and District Development Council members.

DEAP training is done in villages in the pilot districts and involves village and district council officials in practical user-oriented assessment methodologies and action planning techniques using PRA, mapping and other local-level techniques.

## 5 Implementation and Results

*Implementing the NCS*

The National Conservation Strategy document recommended the creation of an inter-ministerial committee to monitor implementation of the strategy. This committee was established in 1990 and was chaired by the Deputy Secretary of the Ministry of Environment and Tourism with representatives from the Ministries of Lands, Agriculture and Water Development, Local Government, Rural and Urban Development, Transport and Energy, Finance, Economic Planning and Development, Health, and Community Development and Women's Affairs.

There was a delay between publishing the strategy document in 1987 and forming the committee to oversee implementation in 1990. This was due to several factors. These included the absence of Cabinet approval and a lack of mandate for implementation. With these outstanding, there was no momentum from decision-makers in government. Second, without an implementation plan detailing the respective responsibilities for action, it was unclear how to move the strategy forward. As a result, pressure to implement the ideas in the strategy document has come largely from outside government, from national NGOs such as ENDA and ZERO, together with academic and community leaders who originally participated in preparation of the strategy.

Since its formation, the inter-ministerial Strategy Implementation Committee has commissioned a review of environmental and resource-use legislation in Zimbabwe which was completed in 1990. The Committee has also recommended the formulation of action plans for implementing the strategy, including identification of specific responsibilities for actions, budgets, and comprehensive participation by districts and provinces.

Although the NCS document has not been fully realized, selected aspects of the strategy have been successfully implemented since the document was published in 1987. Notable examples are the creation of the new Ministry of Environment and Tourism in 1990; a shift in policy from a law enforcement approach to the promotion of conservation education and awareness; land reclamation activities (including gully reclamation and reforestation instituted to rehabilitate degraded communal lands); and a new policy of 'growth with sustainability' which was adopted by the Ministry of Finance to promote sustainable economic growth.

Environmental impact assessment (EIA) has also been adopted as a government requirement before any major project can proceed. Specific EIA guidelines and EIA legislation have yet to be developed, although these tasks are part of the work plan of the Environmental Planning and Coordination Unit in the Ministry of Environment and Tourism.

Current activities include planning workshops on EIA and environmental economics, the development of EIA guidelines, and a review of existing legislation which will lead to recommendations for new omnibus environmental management legislation. Close linkages between the Ministry of Environment and Tourism and the Planning Commission are being developed in carrying out these activities.

*Implementing the DEAP*

The DEAP process has invigorated the implementation of the NCS, largely through the participatory nature of the process at the community level. The DEAP has assisted villagers to identify their own problems and needs, and, through an action planning process, to identify solutions which are reflected in DESs. Most importantly, DEAP stresses that which villagers can do for themselves, without the additional input of government or aid agencies. It tries to encourage self-reliance and reduce dependence on aid and government.

The assessment or diagnostic phase, carried out with intensive use of participatory rural appraisal (PRA), leads to an action planning phase and then to the implementation of small projects at the village level. These are carried out by the villagers themselves, with governmental technical support and advice when necessary.

The DEAP process has trained a Core Team of eight professionals who have subsequently trained District Strategy Teams in four of the pilot districts. In 1997 the remaining four districts will go through the same training. The Ministry of Environment in Zimbabwe would like to see the DEAP process as a fully operational national programme covering all districts in Zimbabwe. It will take a considerable investment in training and demonstration activities in order for villagers to feel the benefits of the process.

### Institutional Arrangements

The NCS remains housed in the Ministry of Environment and Tourism, and the DEAP is implemented by the Department of Natural Resources, a division of the Ministry of Environment and Tourism. At the district level, a DEAP team is comprised of staff from different ministries, such as Land and Water Resources Development, Agriculture, Local Government, Rural and Urban Development, and Health. It is through these district teams working together in the field that the linkage and dialogue between different ministries occur. National links between ministries remain weak, however.

### Integration and Harmonization

At the national level the NCS is still the main strategic environmental framework in Zimbabwe. Since it is outdated and has many gaps, an updated NCS is badly

needed and is likely to be undertaken as part of the NEAP for Zimbabwe.

At the district level the DEAP is intended to act as an integrating force for new strategic initiatives; existing processes like CAMPFIRE and Africa 2000 will link with the DEAP process to provide an integrated local-level resource management and planning framework. This integration is still in the planning stages.

### Capacity Development

Capacity development is one of the main strengths of the DEAP. The DEAP process requires training of government and NGO staff in participatory techniques, assessment methods, planning action, and facilitation techniques. The majority of training is done in villages in each of the pilot districts with villagers and district council representatives. The Core Team stays in villages for the duration of the first and second assessments (for an average time of 15 days).

Training moves through a number of phases. In each pilot district, the Core Team and District Strategy Team (DST) start with a first sustainability assessment, meeting with community members, leaders and RDCs in each pilot district. The assessment process reveals the villagers' perceptions of their well-being and that of their environment and their

views of problems, both causes and effects.
It also shows what they wish their
environment and lives to be like, and their
ideas for a strategy to reach this vision.

The Core Team and District Strategy
Team then report back to the District
Development Council (DDC) on the
results of the sustainability assessment,
highlighting the key issues, problems and
solutions perceived by communities.
Second assessments are then carried out in
each pilot district to take analysis further.
They evaluate institutional strengths and
weaknesses in the district, and refine the
strategy that emerged from the first
assessment. Indicators of ecosystem and
human well-being are identified by
community members; these are used as a
monitoring and assessment tool for the
villagers themselves and by district
officials. Existing district initiatives and
investments are analyzed to see how they
meet the needs identified, how they can
be better utilized and which additional
resources are needed.

The District Environmental Strategy is
developed and refined by the District
Strategy Team, highlighting key issues,
problems and solutions, and priorities. A
'pyramid-of-action' identifies activities
that people can undertake without
assistance, actions they can take with
assistance, and actions that others have to
take. Terms of Reference are developed

with the RDCs and DDCs for the
demonstration projects to be established
in each district. Key demonstration
activities are funded and implemented at
the district level through existing DEAP
funds for initiating longer term programmes. Long-term action programmes
are developed and taken to donors and the
Government of Zimbabwe.

*Communications*

A full communications strategy for the
DEAP pilot phase is still in preparation,
although documentation of the experience
and learning from DEAP has begun. The
process at the village level is being recor-
ded in slides and video for subsequent
training and dissemination. A brochure
describing the process has been published
and widely distributed. A PRA video
documentary is being considered for
training and awareness purposes.

*Monitoring and Evaluation*

To date there has been no monitoring or
evaluation of the NCS. However, the
Ministry of Environment and Tourism
has proposed that M&E of projects
carried out under the action plans be
undertaken at the district or provincial
level, where projects are implemented.

Monitoring, reflection, evaluation and
refocusing of activities play a critical role

in the DEAP process. DEAP is built around an assessment process that produces indicators of human and ecosystem well-being. These are used to monitor progress and adapt the strategy to changing circumstances. In the initial stages of DEAP, monitoring and evaluation focuses on the development of methods to assess the situation and needs at the village and ward levels, and to develop local strategies in a participatory way.

## 6 Lessons Learned

In retrospect, the major shortcomings of the Zimbabwe NCS process have been as follows:

- the lack of an implementation framework and action plans detailing responsibilities and budgets; and
- the lack of integration of the strategy process with key economic and development planning processes. It has not been able to compete for government attention with the post-war priorities of reconstruction, food security, rural development and, most recently, drought relief.

Factors encouraging the strategy process have included the recognition on the part of resource managers of the need for an integrated approach to conservation planning, as well as Zimbabwe's participation in the launch of the World Conservation Strategy. In addition, the negative environmental effects of the prolonged civil war acted as a motivating factor for action on the part of natural resource managers and NGOs.

The development of Zimbabwe's NCS process illustrates the critical need for strategies to be well integrated with national economic and development planning processes through effective institutional mechanisms. Despite a committed effort on the part of natural resource managers, the NCS has remained well outside key economic and development planning processes and policies. Consequently, the strategy document was never debated in Parliament or adopted by Cabinet. Even though there was early political commitment to the formulation of the strategy, it could not be sustained in light of other national priorities.

The absence of NCS implementation action plans specifying priorities, responsibilities and budgetary requirements created a climate of uncertainty as to how to move forward with the NCS. This contributed significantly to the delay in implementation.

The DEAP process has also generated lessons, even in the pilot phase:

- a multi-disciplinary DEAP Core Team is likely to be more effective than conventional sector teams for resource management and action planning at the local level, since a range of perspectives will be represented;
- the involvement and active participation of local communities and authorities in the decision-making process of DEAPs has resulted in a sense of community ownership of the process and empowerment to take action without outside assistance;
- the bottom-up approach of DEAP must eventually link with national top-down processes or they will be isolated and will fail to influence national agendas;
- the admission by civil servants that the top-down approach commonly used by governments has not yielded significant sustainable achievements is a positive step and opens up the dialogue for new ideas and experiments in action planning and implementation; and
- the need for environmental legislation and policy reform in Zimbabwe has enabled environmental institutions to address current environmental and development issues highlighted in Agenda 21 as well as in the national papers to UNCED and the Zimbabwe State of the Environment Report.

## 7 *Chronology*

**1980**
Zimbabwe gains independence after prolonged civil war of more than a decade; Robert Mugabe leads the ZANU one-party government. Zimbabwe participates in the launch of the World Conservation Strategy.

**1983**
Formation of a committee to oversee the preparation of an NCS.

**1984–85**
Gro Brundtland, Chair of the World Commission on Environment and Development invites Bernard Chidzero, Minister of Finance for Zimbabwe, to serve on the WCED; WCED Report released (1985).

**1986**
Zimbabwe delegation attends the WCS Conference in Ottawa. The Ministry of Natural Resources and the NCS Committee undertake the drafting of the Zimbabwe National Conservation Strategy document.

**1987**
The NCS document, "Zimbabwe's Road to Survival", is published by the Ministry of Natural Resources and Tourism.

**1990**
A new Ministry of Environment and Tourism is established; an Environmental Planning and Coordination Unit is created in the ministry responsible for NCS implementation. An inter-ministerial committee to monitor strategy implementation is established. Resource-use legislation is reviewed with a view to amendments for improved environmental management.

**1991**
Second National Five-Year Plan (1991–95) refers to the importance of the environment to economic well-being and makes a policy commitment to environmental impact assessment for development projects.

**1992**
A national conference is held in response to Agenda 21; recommendations from the conference form the priorities for an Environmental Action Plan.

**1993**
Zimbabwe undertakes the preparation of NCS action planning, incorporating relevant aspects of Agenda 21.

**1994**
DEAP Phase is conceived as the implementation phase of the NCS. Planning for the DEAP pilot phase is completed and its implementation agreed on.

**1995**
DEAP pilot phase starts at the village level in eight pilot districts.

**1996**
Ministry indicates wish for DEAP to become a national programme and training programme expands.

| | |
|---|---|
| AFTEN | African Environmental Division (World Bank) |
| AGENDA 21 | Statement of principles and action plan for sustainable development, from the 1992 Earth Summit in Rio |
| ASAL | Arid and Semi-arid Lands |
| CAPAE | Cellule d'appui au plan d'action environnemental |
| CDC | Conservation for Development Centre |
| CEMF | Community Environment Microproject Fund |
| CFSCD | Community Forest and Soil Conservation Department |
| CIDA | Canadian International Development Association |
| CITES | Convention on International Trade in Endangered Species |
| CMC | Conservation Monitoring Centre |
| DANIDA | Danish International Development Agency |
| DEAP | District Environmental Action Plan |
| DREA | Department of Research and Environmental Affairs |
| DS-EAP | District Specific Environmental Action Plan |
| EA | Environmental Assessment |
| EAE | Eritrean Agency for the Environment |
| EAP | Environmental Action Plan |
| ECZ | Environmental Council of Zambia |
| EEC | European Economic Community |
| EFAP | Ethiopian Forestry Action Plan |
| EIA | Environmental Impact Assessment |
| EP&D | (Ministry of) Environmental Planning and Development |
| EPU | Environmental Planning Unit |
| ESP | Environmental Support Programme |
| EVDSA | Ethopian Valleys Development Studies Authority |
| FAO | Food and Agriculture Organization |
| FEPA | Federal Environmental Protection Agency |
| FINNIDA | Finnish International Development Agency |
| FZS | Frankfurt Zoological Society |
| GNP | Gross National Product |

*185*

| | | | | |
|---|---|---|---|---|
| GOK | Government of Kenya | MRDASW | Ministry of Reclamation and Development of Arid, Semi-arid areas and Wastelands |
| GTZ | Deutsche Gelleschaft für Technische Zusammenarbeit | MTNRE | Ministry of Tourism, Natural Resources and the Environment |
| HUZA | Human Settlements of Zambia | MWEMEP | Ministry of Water, Energy, Minerals and Environmental Protection |
| IDA | International Development Association | NACCR | National Advisory Committee on Conservation of Renewable Resources |
| IIED | International Institute for Environment and Development | | |
| IMF | International Monetary Fund | NARESCON | Natural Resources Conservation Council |
| IUCN | World Conservation Union | | |
| KWS | Kenya Wildlife Service | NCC | National Conservation Committee |
| LPG | Liquid petroleum gas | | |
| MEDAC | Ministry of Economic Development and Cooperation | NCDP | National Commission for Development Planning |
| MENR | Ministry of Environment and Natural Resources | NCE | National Committee for the Environment |
| MEP | Ministry of Environmental Protection | NCS | National Conservation Strategy |
| MLNR | Ministry of Lands and Natural Resources | NCSS | National Conservation Strategy Secretariat |
| MoNRDEP | Ministry of Natural Resource Development and Environmental Protection | NCSSD | National Conservation Strategy for Sustainable Development |
| MoPED | Ministry of Planning and Economic Development | NEAP | National Environmental Action Plan |
| MOREA | Ministry of Research and Environmental Affairs | NEC | National Environmental Council |

| | | | | |
|---|---|---|---|---|
| NEMA | National Environmental Management Authority | | PEAP | Provincial Environmental Action Plan |
| NEMC | National Environmental Management Council | | PRA | Participatory Rural Appraisal |
| NEMP-E | National Environmental Management Plan for Eritrea | | PTC | Planning and Technical Committee |
| NEP | National Environmental Policy | | RCS | Regional Conservation Strategy |
| NEPA | National Environmental Protection Authority | | REAP | Regional Environmental Action Plan |
| NES | National Environment Secretariat | | RECC | Regional Environmental Coordinating Committee |
| NGO | Non-governmental Organization | | SIDA | Swedish International Development Authority |
| NORAD | Norwegian Agency for International Development | | SRCS | Serengeti Regional Conservation Strategy |
| NRCC | Natural Resources Conservation Council | | SWRI | Serengeti Wildlife Research Institute |
| NRHSD | Natural Resources and Human Settlement Department | | TANAPA | Tanzanian National Parks |
| | | | TCGE | Technical Consultative Group on Environment |
| NRM | National Resistance Movement | | TFAP | Tropical Forestry Action Plan |
| OAU | Organization of African Unity | | TGE | Transitional Government of Ethiopia |
| ODA | Official Development Assistance | | UK | United Kingdom |
| ONCCP | Office of the National Committee for Central Planning | | UNCED | United Nations Conference on Environment and Development |
| | | | UNDP | United Nations Development Programme |

| | | | | |
|---|---|---|---|---|
| UNEP | United Nations Environment Programme | WCS | World Conservation Strategy | |
| UNESCO | United Nations Educational, Scientific and Cultural Organization | WEAP | Ward Environmental Action Plan | |
| | | WEMEP | Ministry of Water, Energy, Minerals and Environmental Protection | |
| UNSO | United Nations Sudano-Sahelian Office | | | |
| UNZA | University of Zambia | WRI | World Resources Institute | |
| USAID | United Nations Agency for International Development | WWF | Worldwide Fund For Nature | |
| VEAP | Village Environmental Action Plan | ZECC | Zonal Environmental Coordinating Committee | |

UNIVERSITY OF GREENWICH LIBRARY